LAN
RA

Countryside Books' walking guides cover most areas of England and Wales and include the following series:

County Rambles
Walks for Motorists
Exploring Long Distance Paths
Literary Walks
Pub Walks

A complete list is available from the publishers:

3 Catherine Road, Newbury, Berkshire

LANCASHIRE RAMBLES

Fourteen Country Walks
around Lancashire

Alan Shepley

———————

With Historical Notes

COUNTRYSIDE BOOKS
NEWBURY, BERKSHIRE

COUNTRYSIDE BOOKS
3 Catherine Road
Newbury, Berkshire

ISBN 1 85306 177 8

Cover photograph of the road through Bowland Forest
taken by Bill Meadows

Produced through MRM Associates Ltd., Reading
Typeset by Wessex Press Design & Print Ltd., Warminster
Printed in England by J. W. Arrowsmith Ltd., Bristol

Contents

Introduction

Even Lancastrians, born and bred, would admit that the county hides its countryside delights under a bushel. A high proportion of those who enter its boundaries do so only for work or to exit again, at some speed, on one of the motorways. Either way you are missing some of the best walking in the north of England.

The present boundaries are, of course, not those of the old County Palatine. The changes of 1974 saw both gains and losses; the Forest of Bowland was a clear gain, Furness — Lancashire across the Sands — a great loss. Many living within the old boundaries still consider themselves most definitely as Lancastrians and I hope they will forgive the practical decision to include in this book only walks within the present county.

The eastern half of the county, poor hill land for the most part, is formed of grits, sandstones and shales, lying on top of the coal measures. In the Ribble Valley and northwards limestones appear and the Arnside and Silverdale area at the northern tip of the county is entirely made of them. The west consists mainly of two coastal plains, the Fylde north of the Ribble, and the West Lancashire Mosses to the south. Both areas have extensive coverings of glacial sands, clays and gravels as well as peatlands and silt with smaller areas of younger reddish sandstone outcrops. This plain is really an extension of lowland Midland England, squeezed between the mountains and the sea.

Rock and landform have determined much of Lancashire's history. Before the Romans came the only practicable land to live on seems to have been beside the sea and in the hills. Romans and Normans made little difference to this pattern and their strongholds, like Lancaster itself, and their roads had to hug the base of the hills. From Domesday to Tudor times, Lancashire was clearly regarded as poor land and life couldn't change much until the mosses were drained and the water power of the valleys beneath the rainy hills became a basis for the start of the industrial revolution. The relative availability of coal and stone, and a suitable climate for spinning and weaving, has ensured that the consequent industry became Lancashire's image well into this century. Meanwhile, a lot of lowland Lancashire was developed into rich agricultural land once access to markets became possible.

The walks in this book range across the county and, therefore, will bring you into contact with most aspects of it. The routes vary in length and difficulty and, in some cases where crossing wild open moorland, will require you to carry a compass and know how to use it. The accompanying sketch maps should ensure that, together with the walk descriptions, you have little difficulty in finding your way. Major route-finding features are indicated by symbols a key to which is given on page 8. Although all routes have been re-walked, details on the ground do change and carrying the appropriate Ordnance Survey map is recommended so that alternatives can be identified if need arises. In addition, the OS map also carries a great deal of information about other things nearby which may also be of interest to you or which available space has prevented me including. The OS sheets are listed for each walk; Landranger 1:50.000 and 1:25.000 Pathfinder. National Grid References have been quoted to 6 figures, ie the nearest 100 metres in the form GR 123456 (the walks covered are all within GR letter square SD).

A book of walks is never, truly, an individual effort. Over the years I have walked much of Lancashire in the company of many friends, too numerous to mention, whose keen eyes have often seen what I had missed. Many before me have written of their own favourite walks and have set me off on exciting paths. I acknowledge my great debt to them all and apologise for unwittingly putting my boot on anyone's toes!

INTRODUCTION

In recent years, local authorities have taken a much more positive approach to the value of our footpath heritage as part of everyone's recreational resource. Mostly I find Lancashire passably signed and stiled. On rare occasions this has not been so and I have tried to indicate in the descriptions where there were problems when I last passed that way. Do make sure the local authority is told if you should find your access barred or the way impracticable; it is one way of making certain that the Countryside Commission aim of having all our Rights of Way fully open by the turn of the century is realised.

Alan Shepley
March 1992

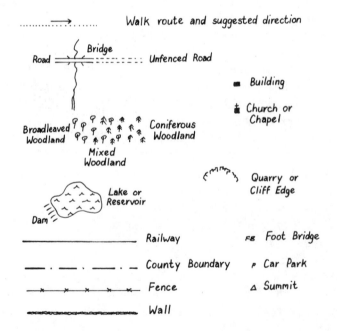

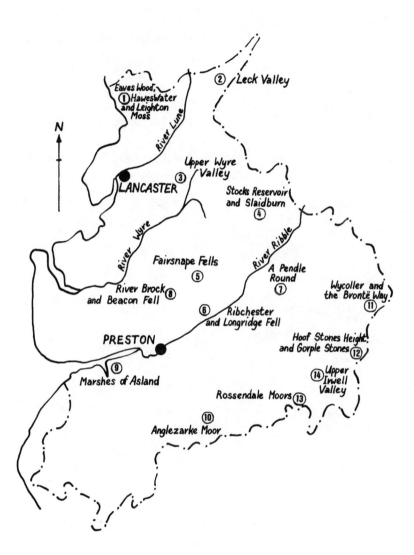

Area map showing locations of the walks

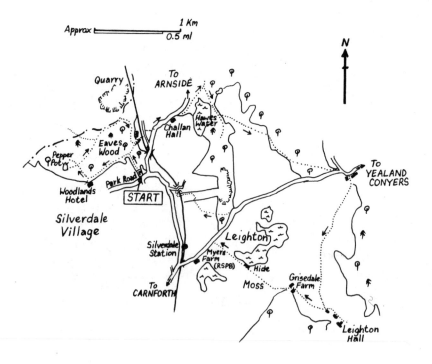

Eaves Wood, Hawes Water and Leighton Moss

Introduction: The subtle and intimate beauty of this smallscale landscape was recognised by its designation in 1972 as an Area of Outstanding Natural Beauty covering about 75 square km (rather under 29 square miles). About half of the stubby peninsula of limestone, which juts into Morecambe Bay between the rivers Kent and Keer, is in Lancashire. This walk begins in the delightful mixed woodland of Eaves Wood, with exceptional views from the 'Pepper Pot' of Morecambe Bay and around to Clougha Pike. It then skirts Hawes Water, one of only two natural lakes in the county, before continuing to the RSPB Reserve at Leighton Moss, where you may be lucky enough to see deer or otters as well as many varieties of birds. The area is heavily wooded and has a feeling of comparative remoteness which belies its closeness to the main modern routes north to Scotland.

Distance: A gentle 7.2 km (4.5 miles) easily walked in half a day. Maps — OS Landranger 97, OS Pathfinder 636.

Refreshments: Silverdale village has several choices and the RSPB centre at Leighton Moss serves snacks. More substantial meals are obtainable around the corner at the former station house, now renamed 'Coppernobs'.

How to get there: Start from the National Trust car park on Park Road, Silverdale, opposite The Row ½ mile north of

Silverdale station, reached from the A6 via Arnside or Carnforth (GR 472759).

The Walk: Follow the path into Eaves Wood to a T-junction and turn left. The path rises along the edge of the wood. After about five minutes, fork right. Shortly you pass the Woodlands Hotel and should bear uphill to the right.

Climb up King William's Hill, rising quickly through hazel coppice and amongst some impressive yews. At the top is a crossing of the main path along the top of the hill. Detour hard left for a couple of minutes to emerge at the 'Pepper Pot' on Castlebarrow, built in 1887 to commemorate Queen Victoria's Jubilee. The view on a clear day is dramatic from the sands of Morecambe Bay to Clougha Pike to the east, behind Lancaster: Silverdale village is spread out below. Return to the junction of paths and continue directly ahead along the hill with a low limestone cliff on your left.

In two minutes you reach a gap in a wall. Pass through and immediately go left and up some steps to come into an open area of woodland. This is criss-crossed with many small paths but the main one continues to be well-defined. At the second broad clearing there is the choice of turning left to go through a stile in the wall (the Cumbria boundary) and to continue across a limestone pavement and down to Arnside Tower. The main path gradually descends and approaches Middlebarrow Quarry, the noise of which will be heard clearly on weekdays. Just short of the quarry the path steepens. Bear left through a wall and walk ahead to cross the access drive of Waterslack Garden Centre to the right of the car park and use the stile in the left-hand corner of this field to reach the railway line.

Cross the line with care and take equal care on the lane for this is the main access to the quarry. Walk left ten paces and take a gate in the hedge on the right to go up the bank and across the field to a stile to join the Beetham road (some alternative car parking is to be found here). Here is the first of several views back to the quarry which show its size with the height of Arnside Knott behind. Walk left for about 300 metres to pass Challan Hall (bed and breakfast for the supremely weary!). The field to the north contains a massive, detached block of limestone known as the Buck Stone. Just beyond, a track forks right into the wood (this is one of three places on the walk where there is no Public Footpath sign at the roadside). Follow this amongst some fine broad-leaved trees close to the edge of Hawes Water (reputedly one of only two natural lakes left in the county: the other is Martin Mere near Burscough).

Walk around an open area at the head of the lake which was probably the site from which clay was won for the local pottery industry in the late Middle Ages. At the end of the wood cross the stream which runs from a small tarn inside the Gait Barrows National Nature Reserve. Beside the stile is an information notice and a map. Bear diagonally right across the field from the middle of which you have a good view across the majority of the reserve. The limestone pavement shows up well surrounded by the old coppice woodlands, from which came much of the wood to make the charcoal to fire the former Leighton iron-smelting furnace which lay on the far side of these woods, beside the beck which forms the county boundary.

At the far field boundary use a stile by the gate to join a track to the right through the scrub thorn of Yealand Hall Allotment. The RSPB reserve at Leighton Moss is now in sight below and the view opens out to the Bay beyond. Five more minutes will bring you to the Y-junction of roads at Yealand Storrs. Just around the corner to the left is space for a couple of cars to be parked by the roadside.

Cross the road and walk ahead towards the house and cottages on the right. Beside the double gates is a small wooden gate in the wall leading onto a footpath which crosses in front of the house and barn and enters a field. Follow the track and bear right to walk beside the wall and hedge along five fields to come out on a lane opposite the house at Leighton Hall Home Farm. Down on your right is Storrs Moss where a Neolithic settlement has been found in the peat. At the farm you have the choice to turn up the hill and walk the short distance to Leighton Hall. Otherwise, turn right down the hill to go through Grisedale Farm. Take the right fork of the track alongside the barn about 50 metres on into the field (the barn at the far side of the field carries several notices making it clear that the gate there is not the path!) and drop down to enter the RSPB reserve.

The bridleway here crosses the centre of the reserve with a freely accessible public hide about two-thirds of the way along on the right; an annexe to this has facilities for the disabled. Within the hide, and on posts along the track, is information about the wildlife of the reserve. Most people come here to watch the birds but there are resident otters and, on a day in autumn when I walked through, a roe doe casually grazed at the edge of the reeds within 10 metres of me.

At the road the walk continues to the right but you may, by now, want some refreshment or to visit the shop and displays at the RSPB centre at Myers Farm about five minutes along to the left.

Return to the junction of track and road (where the only sign reads 'No parking beyond this point') and continue on. At 50 metres on the left there is a footpath sign to Red Bridge. I suggest you ignore this and walk on through the wood (where there is some roadside parking) almost to the other side. On the left is a set of old limestone steps about 20 metres short of the field gate. Once again there is no sign here but go up the steps and keep to the left to cross the wood diagonally to a squeeze-stile through the far wall. Just beyond the wall you cross 'The Trough', a natural feature which can be traced for about 5 km northwards (you crossed a less evident part of it beside Hawes Water). It marks a fault in the rock with sides up to 18 metres in places; part of the wood has disappeared as Trowbarrow Quarries were dug. In times of Scots invasions down this coast there is no doubt it formed an ideal place for the locals to hide both themselves and their beasts.

Continue diagonally to the right across the field past an oak tree to a stile in the right-hand corner (which is where you rejoin the alternative path to Red Bridge). The view to the left across the Moss and out to the Bay is most attractive. There is another stile in the next wall behind the large boulder in front of you. Once through this you reach a track and should turn right and left in 10 metres to follow a narrow path to the far side of the trees, and left along the wall to dip into a little gully and emerge on the track again in an abandoned quarry. Cross directly ahead and recross the railway. Turn immediately right up a bank to reach a lane opposite a house called 'The Barn' at Red Bridge.

Fifty metres left will bring you to the main road. Turn right here and walk along the verge for about 300 metres to the end of Park Road close by the car park.

Historical Notes

Eaves Wood: The Woodlands Hotel is just the present guise of a house known in the early 1800s as Hill House. It was owned by Thomas Inman who was involved in the Liverpool shipping trade; the first part of the path is still called Inman Road. In 1929 the then owner of the house gave 23 acres, including Castlebarrow, to the National Trust. Since then more than 100 acres have been added in various ways to form the property now called Eaves Wood. The woodland is very mixed in character. Some is relatively ancient and undisturbed with yew, oak and lime on deeper soils. There is

15

some relatively old planting of beech and hornbeam, and small plantations of larch and Scots pine are to be found. In places the trees have been coppiced — especially ash and hazel — on quite a short rotation of perhaps 12 to 16 years to provide a wide range of sizes of material (small enough for pea sticks and large enough for brush heads) including wood for charcoal making.

RSPB reserve: The reserve proper is about 320 acres of reed beds and open water and has an international reputation for bird life. The Centre at Myers Farm, where binoculars can be hired, charts sightings of interest daily. In addition to the public hide on the route there are further ones on the shore of the Bay (GR 476734). Access elsewhere is by permit only, available at the Centre, and a programme of guided walks and evening talks is offered. Note the Centre is closed on Tuesdays and on Christmas Day and Boxing Day (GR 478751). Tel Silverdale (0524) 701601.

Leighton Hall: The Hall as you see it now is basically a rebuilding of about 1760 on a old (1200s) site after damage during the Jacobite risings. It was 'gothicised' by Richard Gillow, of the furniture-making family of Lancaster, around 1822. The tower and the south wing were built to the designs of Paley and Austin in 1870. The inside is very fine with a collection of original Gillow furniture and interesting paintings, silver and clocks. It is open May to September inclusive 2 pm to 5 pm on Sunday, Wednesday and Thursday — the grounds only on Tuesday and Friday. A display of free-flying birds of prey is given at 3.30 pm in suitable weather on each day the grounds are open. Road access is well signed (GR 494796). Tel Carnforth (0524) 734474.

The Leck Valley

Introduction: The valley of the river Leck is another of those bonuses which Lancashire hides away. Not only does it hold a surprising variety and interest but it's a surprise it's in Lancashire at all! Travelling the A65 you expect to cross from North Yorkshire direct into Cumbria and the signs which mark the boundary of the 'City of Lancaster', halfway between Ingleton and Kirkby Lonsdale and just short of the crossing of the river Lune, are most unexpected. The county includes the whole of the south-eastern slope of the valley and the north-western slope from the junction of the Leck and Lune to about halfway up; thereafter the boundary is in the valley bottom in what has become Ease Gill.

The walk follows the Leck up the valley towards Ease Gill, where the slopes conceal an interlinked system of caves over 30 km (20 miles) in extent. Access to the caves themselves is on private land and strictly controlled, but walkers can see one of the resurgences at Leck Beck Head. Returning to Cowan Bridge, past an attractive waterfall, the ramble continues by passing the school where the Brontë sisters briefly attended and skirts the site of a Roman fort.

Distance: By using 50 metres of the A65 at Cowan Bridge the walk described can be made a figure of eight, or two loops. Above Cowan Bridge is 11 km (6.5 miles), below is 6.1 km (3.5 miles); so there is a choice for either a half day or full day. The upper valley is wild and isolated and it is wise to be prepared for bad weather. Maps — OS Landranger 97 & 98 , OS Pathfinder 628.

17

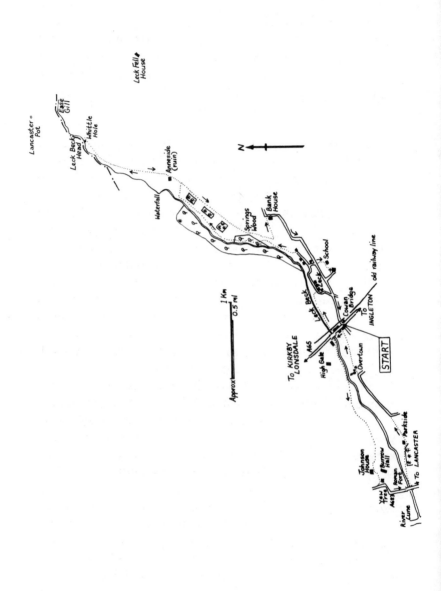

Refreshments: 5 km (about 3 miles), in either direction, along the A65 will bring you to a very wide choice of possibilities in either Kirkby Lonsdale or Ingleton. At Cowan Bridge there are two restaurants; The Cobwebs and at the Hipping Hall Hotel. A mile towards Kirkby Lonsdale is the Whoop Hall Inn and at Burrow is the Railwayman pub.

How to get there: Use the A65 to Cowan Bridge and turn east at the crossroads to park outside the village hall behind the post office (GR 636765).

The Walk: Return to the A65 and use the stile on the right before the river bridge. Follow the fence line under the old railway arch and along the river bank until the first houses of Leck village appear on your right and use the track to join the lane at the corner beside them. OS maps still show a bridge across the river: its remains indicate the power of this stream in winter flood! Walk ahead up the lane through the scattered hamlet beside walls of rounded beck stones and past peacocks, Canada geese and goats, to the farm at the end. Take the left-hand track nearest the river.

The route follows close to the river for 1½ miles, passing through the aptly-named Springs Wood on the way with the remains of another footbridge close to its far boundary. In the appropriate season this land is shot over and you will probably find many spent cartridges about and tags marking the shooters' stands; in the far field you pass close to a cabin.

Past the second spruce plantation on the right the fields give way to coarser grasses, rushes and bracken. Cross the side stream and make immediately right, up the bank, to join a well-marked track and go left to the ruined farm at Anneside. The public path goes straight ahead here, parallel to the wall on the right but the area is open with many sheep trods. Follow the path to meet the river again at Leck Beck Head where the county boundary now runs half right up the

19

stream in Ease Gill. In clear weather the small scars of limestone marking the cave-rich area upslope from you are easily picked out and, from some points, the stone pillars of The Three Men of Gragareth break the skyline of the heather moorland to the north-east, just short of the boundary of the Yorkshire Dales National Park.

With permission, it is possible to explore the area up towards Leck Fell House, above the limestone scars. Otherwise, retrace your steps to Anneside. The river has created an incised meander here, with a pleasant waterfall, and it is obvious that others have been to view it before, even though it is not strictly on the path.

Use the track, now, to return along the valley side by the wall above the plantations. I was joined here by a quite unconcerned red squirrel, scampering along the top of it. From above Springs Wood the view opens out down the valley and over Leck and Cowan Bridge towards the Lune. Drop down the field and just before the gate of a narrow, walled enclosure turn back upslope to the left (GR 647774) to exit onto the lane left of Bank House farm.

Turn right and go down the lane to the crossroads signed left to the school. Walk round the school buildings on the right and cross the field to enter the churchyard of St Peter's (there is alternative parking here). Out of the gate turn right and then left to reach Cowan Bridge again in five minutes.

The second loop begins on the far side of the river bridge in front of a building on which a plaque records that the Brontë sisters spent some of their schooldays here. Below the parapet the path runs above an old fish run and along the river bank to join the track to High Gale. The footbridge just beyond still stands but bears the legend 'Weak bridge; no more than two persons at one time'. Do not cross, but go right over the stile before the cattle grid and diagonally left to a gate beside the hedge of the garden of Low Gale to reach a stone and wood footbridge over the beck just beyond. Bear slightly left and follow a faint track to pick up an old hedge line and go left along it and down to some newly planted trees in a small, boggy triangle of land.

The stile over the end of the wall brings Burrow Hall into view for the first time. Join the track by the wall on the left to pass a barn and cross a ford by a footbridge to reach Johnson House farm, dated 1680. Emerge onto the main road behind Yew Tree farm at Keeper's Cottage. Care is needed when walking around the bends to the left for the road is narrow and there are double white lines. Just around the bends the field to the left is occupied by the remains of a Roman fort, though they are all grassed over. Walk down the road to the bridge inscribed with the names of the Supervisors of 1733 and 1735, and a tasteful note that it was rewidened in 1968.

Cross and use the stile to return up the opposite bank of the river. The path goes into the yard of Parkside farm on the right just beyond the plantation and left across the yard and ahead through the field to join a lane at a right-angled bend. Follow the lane less than ½ mile to Overtown and go straight ahead to the white cottages. Use the stile on their immediate left to continue through the fields to reach the A65 by the bus stop in Cowan Bridge, at which point is the one and only footpath sign on the whole route! Turn right and left to return to the car park.

Historical notes

The Brontës: Just north of the bridge on the A65 at Cowan Bridge is the building which housed the school for clergymen's daughters, founded by Rev Wilson, vicar of Tunstall, in 1824. In 1824 and 1825 Maria, Elizabeth, Charlotte and Emily Brontë attended the school in, it seems, an atmosphere of some unhappiness. The school itself moved to Casterton, just across the Cumbria boundary, in 1833 and still flourishes.

21

Shuttleworth Estates: The upper Leck Valley forms part of the Shuttleworth Estates and access on the south-western slope of the valley is controlled. Enquiries can be made at the Estate Office, just round the corner towards Leck from Cowan Bridge post office. Tel 05242-71445.

Caving: The areas below Leck Fell House, in the bottom of Ease Gill, and between Bull Pot farm and Ease Gill are riddled with caves of varying difficulty, much of which forms one interlinked system over 20 miles in total extent. A chance lunch beside what turned out to be the entrance to Lancaster Pot, on the Cumbria side, one day in 1946 led to a great expansion of the already known systems. Non-cavers can see the resurgence at Leck Beck Head from the end of the path and are, at that point, standing above the short cave of Whittle Hole. Access to the caves on private land is controlled through the Council of Northern Caving Clubs and a notice posted at Bank House farm (GR 651774) gives current details of how to make contact. Entry to the caves is hazardous and should be made only with permission, experienced leadership and the correct equipment.

Roman Fort: Not a great deal of the Roman fort at Burrow is to be seen (GR 614756) — just low mounds in the fields between the Leck Beck and the river Lune. Pevsner claims its name to have been Galacum, but this seems to be no more than a guess. Some excavation has been done and it might have been founded as early as the time of the governorship of Agricola in the 1st century AD. It fills the gap between the fort at Lancaster and that on the upper Lune near Tebay. The nearby Burrow Hall was built for Robert Fenwick in the 1730s and is not open to visitors.

The Railway: The five-arched viaduct across the Leck Beck and the girder bridge over the road in Cowan Bridge are part of what remains of works begun by the 'Little' North Western Railway, formed in 1846, but which were completed by the Lancaster and Carlisle Railway. Even while building, the company was taken over by the London and North Western Railway which, as a result, came to meet its greatest rival, the Midland, at Ingleton. The latter built the Settle-Carlisle route and this one effectively became redundant. This section was opened in 1861, and closed to passengers in 1954 and to goods in 1966.

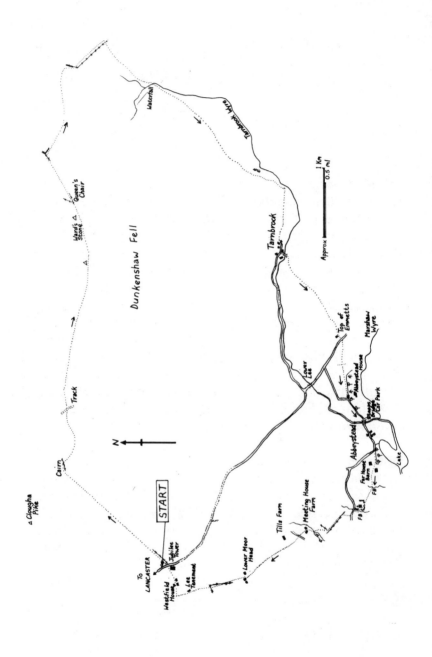

The Upper Wyre Valley

Introduction: This walk makes use of the Access Strip which runs along that marvellous east-west ridge behind Lancaster to the hamlet of Tarnbrook. This dramatic walk begins with wonderful views from the Jubilee Tower on the Trough of Bowland road, before striking out across the open moorland. Up on the wild fellside of Ward's Stone, over 1,800 ft above sea level, you can look out over the whole of Morecambe Bay and towards the Lakes, and round over the Bowland Fells and the Trough, before going on your way over heather and peat. The high ground contrasts with wooded dales and river valleys and there is an everchanging panorama before you. The circuit is completed by following the valley down as far as the attractive hamlet of Abbeystead, still owned by the Earls of Sefton, and returns via the isolated Georgian church of Over Wyresdale.

Distance: Unless you halve the walk by leaving one car at the start and another at Tarnbrook, this is a long day's walk, and is best saved for a spell of fair, settled weather. Poor weather and wet peat underfoot simply obscures the views and makes for slow progress. Compass use may be essential. Total distance is 21.5 km (13.5 miles). Maps — OS Landranger 102, OS Pathfinder 659 & 660.

Refreshments: There are no refreshments available on the route. The nearest are at Brow Top Craft Centre, about 2 km in the Lancaster direction from the start.

How to get there: Start from the Jubilee Tower on the Trough of Bowland road approached either from Lancaster centre or from Dunsop Bridge from the south (GR 542573). Please note that no dogs are allowed within the Access Area.

The Walk: The view from the start is justifiably popular with many and is the reason for there being a handy car park, on the edge of which is an Access Area sign and map. Follow the fence up on a narrow and often wet path to a cairn and pole and an up-and-over stile to the right onto the Access Strip and the top of Grit Fell. By now it is stonier and drier underfoot with plenty of bilberry about and a view of the whole of Morecambe Bay, south Cumbria and the Lakes, the Leven and Kent estuaries, and round to Ingleborough and south over the Trough and the Bowland Fells. The Access Strip is marked here by faded yellow paint on the odd stone and post and shortly crosses an obvious shooters' track before climbing over heather peat about two ft deep towards the trig point on Ward's Stone; 560m (1,836 ft). The better vantage point for the view is, in fact, at Queen's Chair across a small plateau and just right of a second trig point; the highest point of the route at 561m (1,839 ft). The wind-eroded sandstone of the rocks is dramatic and provides an overhang under which you can shelter if need be. On the plateau are some massive peat haggs, well over man height, which suggest that erosion has been extensive here though whether because of changing climate or over-grazing is impossible to say.

Drop down slightly left and cross the fence into the angle (there should be a stile but when I was last there it had been toppled over) and follow the right-hand fence along. A massive erosion channel exposes the weak shales and sandstones below the peat. Where the fence meets an angle of walls take the stile to the right; upper Ribblesdale and Ingleton village are visible to the north. Now follow a sequence of wall-fence-wall on your left until a further stile takes you across on a bearing of about 145° and over eroded peat to a last up-and-over stile on a broad col with extensive stone fields. Now bear right to drop via a line of marker posts to join a track just across the head of a waterfall below a weir on the source of the Tarnbrook Wyre; a relaxing spot for lunch.

As you descend the valley opens and there is a glimpse of the lake at Abbeystead surrounded by woods. The track follows the 'black' side of the fell, covered in heather, which contrasts with the far valley side, grassed and with bracken — the 'white' side. Almost at the bottom of Gables Clough, Jubilee Tower can be seen far to the right on the skyline.

The track meets a footpath just short of Tarnbrook hamlet and there is a small squeeze of parking for a couple of cars by the barn at the gate. Walk right to the green and left between a garden wall and a barn conversion to cross the river and follow the yellow-arrowed path through the fields and over the brow. The whole of the fellside below the ridge on which you walked earlier is now dramatically in full view. It is known as Dunkenshaw Fell.

Bear left of the former farm of Top of Emmetts, and walk across the road and bear right following the yellow arrowed route along a bank to a crossing of paths by a gate. Edge slightly left now towards the wood and exit onto the lane via the orchard and garage entrance of a house (there is actually a footpath sign on the wrong side of the road!). Follow the lane down to Stoops Bridge where there is plenty of alternative car parking and, at the right time of the year, lots of young pheasants foraging from the rearing pens at Abbeystead House. The hamlet is all of a piece, of the 1890s and very attractive.

Pass the school and post office and climb the brow with the lake down on your left. At the top of the wood use the stile on the left and aim to go right of the new barn of Far House Barn and cross diagonally to a gate in the corner. Move ahead on the old hedge line and drop to cross a footbridge over Parsons Brook. Climb diagonally right to a gate in the middle of the wall of Over Wyresdale churchyard. The path oddly cuts the corner of the graveyard and exits left to cross Joshua's Beck on a stone flag and turns right up to the lane.

Go left 50 metres and right at a footpath sign and ahead on an old hedge line to a wire fence. This is one of the few points at which I could find no stile in all my Lancashire wanderings so I suggest you, too, just hop over. Take a last glance up the valley before going left along the fence line until a wire fence comes in from the right. Here, bear due north to cross Gallows Clough at the head of the wood and ahead to a stone stile between the buildings of Meeting House farm. Use the access track to cross a metalled lane and take the footpath gate ahead to follow the right-hand fence and hedges to Lower Moor Head. Cross the farm track to the stile and follow the left-hand boundary to almost the end of the second field where a stile exits left. Continue on the same boundary line to the stile in the corner and ahead to the left of Lee Tenement to join the concrete access road. The occupant here clearly has found a corner in old sandstone sinks. The road bends round to Westfield House (which has local produce for sale) and the right of way climbs the bank to reach Jubilee Tower.

Historical Notes

Bowland Access Areas: The Forest of Bowland Area of Outstanding Natural Beauty was designated in 1964 and covers over 300 square miles. The Access Areas agreed with Lancashire County Council are in several blocks, Clougha and the Tarnbrook Strip being one of them. Over 60 square miles of the main Bowland moorlands remain almost entirely under private estate control. They have remained a thorn in the flesh of those who seek the freedom to roam for very many years and continue to attract mass trespass from time to time. That doyen of walkers, Tom Stephenson, began his walking and writing careers in Bowland and joined in many of the battles which have gained such access as there is.

The Moors: The gritstones and shales of these hills produce an acidic soil poor in plant foods and the relatively high rainfall quickly washes out what there is. As a result, the variety of plants is not great and the bright colours of spring and summer flowers are largely absent, only patches of heather and ling put on a show in early autumn. Much of the moor is wet for a large part of the year and dead plant material accumulates as peat. A large area is covered in Molina, or purple moor grass, which forms tussocks which make for difficult walking. Wavy hair grass (Deschampsia sp.) is to be found in the wetter places along with cotton grass (Eriophorum sp.), with its distinctive white cotton-wool seed heads in late June, and sedges (Carex sp.) and rushes (Juncus sp.). Drier areas with smaller tufts, are probably mat grass (Nardus sp.). Most of the drier open moor is covered in heather, ling, bilberry and crowberry. Overstocking leads to disappearance of these latter.

Abbeystead: The name derives from an early monastic foundation which remained only a short while before moving to Ireland. The house was built in 1886 by the Earls of Sefton, who still own the estate and who also created the attractive hamlet at the same time around one or two rather older buildings. The buildings are in local sandstone and more or less Elizabethan in style.

Over Wyresdale church: The church is Georgian of 1733 with a spire added in 1894; inside is a pulpit dated 1684. It stands in the fields rather away from the hamlet. In common with

29

many country churches, it is now part of a joint parish arrangement.

Jubilee Tower: Built by the owner of Hare Appletree (down the hill) to celebrate Queen Victoria's Jubilee in 1887.

Stocks Reservoir and Slaidburn

Introduction: Eastern Bowland is an interesting mixture of open moorland, plantation and valley farms, with the lovely river Hodder running through it and with the largest reservoir in the north-west of England, beneath the waters of which lies the hamlet of Stocks. Little St James' church was built in 1938 using some of the stone from the now submerged village church. Now part of the Ribble Valley District, this was all Yorkshire before 1974. The area is rather more generously served by footpaths than elsewhere in Bowland and this walk makes good use of them. The walk also visits the 'capital' of this area, the village of Slaidburn, with its 15th century church and Old Grammar School.

Distance: Except for the crossing of the river Hodder above the reservoir (which can be difficult after rain), this is a gentle day of 14 km (8.7 miles) — a diversion to avoid the river crossing addes 3 km (1.8 miles). Maps — OS Landranger 103, OS Pathfinder 660.

Refreshments: Pub and shop are available in Slaidburn.

How to get there: Approach using the B6478 from Clitheroe via Newton and Slaidburn or from the A65 at Long Preston. Turn at the Bowland Forest sign at crossroads by Lower Stoney Bank farm 4.8 km (3 miles) north-east of Slaidburn. Park at the North West Water/Forestry Commission car park at the bend after 2.4 km (1.5 miles); both forest trails and footpath maps are displayed (GR 733565).

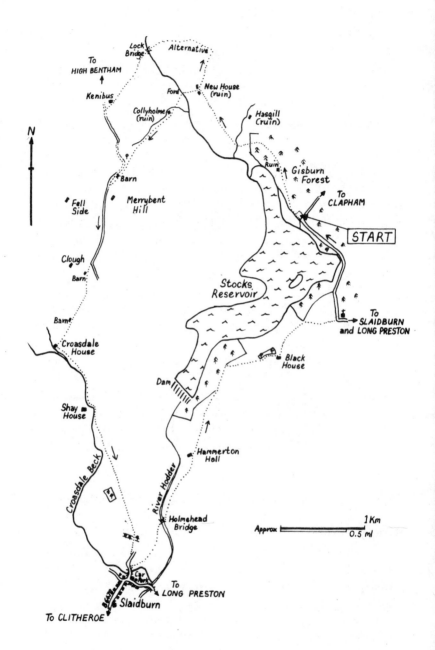

The Walk: Follow red/white trails north-west through a plantation of Norway spruce in which a lot of trees were brought down in the gales of the 1989/90 winter. After you pass a farm ruin and shed, the red/white trails turn off to the right, but continue ahead along the ride (now the line of the public footpath) to the edge of the trees. At the gate into the pasture the view opens out with the reservoir down to the left, the upper Hodder Valley and the fell delightfully called Bloe Greet directly ahead.

The path drops to cross a bridge over the Hasgill Beck with the ruin of Hasgill on the right and clear felled and newly planted areas on the fell above. A track now leads straight up, through poor wet pasture covered in rushes, to the ruin of New House and its barn. For the *main route* take the gates to the left between them and drop down a zigzag track to the old ford over the Hodder. This is an easy crossing when the water is low but impractical after heavy rain. Cross the valley bottom and aim for the lower side of the nearby ruin of Collyhome. Use the gate to gain a path which follows up Copped Hill Clough on your right. This has a series of small waterfalls and holds a narrow wood of alder. The stile halfway may still be broken! Keep close to the stream and cross a track to pass a clump of trees almost at the top of the brow to reach a barn called Brunton Laithe and join the road, unwalled on your side, at the cattle grid.

Debris caught on the rushes in the valley bottom makes it very obvious that the river floods across in times of heavy rain. *After poor weather you should turn right* at New House and take a path up the large field almost to the top boundary. Bear left and drop to the track in Park Clough, descend to the track to Catlow and cross the river by Lock Bridge. Climb up the far side to join the road by Kenibus and walk left to the cattle grid.

From the cattle grid walk down the lane past Merrybent Hill on the left, Fell Side on the right, and turn in the entrance to Clough at the right angled bend after 0.8 km (0.5 miles). Turn left in 50 metres and pass a barn ruin to follow the wall line on your right. Walk ahead over a series of way-marked stiles and past another barn to join the track along the Croasdale Brook close by the front of Croasdale Hall. Follow the track downstream through two fields, turn off to the right at a marked stile by the river and cross to a gate by the bridge to Shay House. The path continues on the same side of the river in a more or less straight line to climb over a smooth, grassed knoll with a walled wood on the right. Aim now for the left-hand end of the large shelterbelt of beech, sycamore and elm and drop down the field on the far side bearing left a little to join the lane on the edge of Slaidburn village.

You will certainly want to look round the village, maybe eat here, or use the toilets at the car park by the river Hodder. (This is an alternative start point for those who would rather take their villages first or last in the day.)

Return to the bridge over the Croasdale Brook (GR 713525) and take the iron kissing gate on the northern side. Walk downstream to join a track which crosses the brook at a paved ford. Turn left and follow the left-hand wall along to cross the river Hodder (dryshod this time!) at the steeply-arched Holmehead Bridge. The path actually uses the grass of the field but you are hardly likely to be told off for joining it by walking along the track all the way. Just before Hammerton Hall the old bridge across a side beck has almost been washed away and a new culvert has been put in.

Pass the Hall, follow the signing round to the right and take the left hand of the two gates with yellow arrows on them. The path is well marked up over Ten Acre Hill. It turns a right angle at the top and clear felling here gives views down to the reservoir just above the dam. Go down now to Black House farm, staying close to the edge of the wood. Take the track left at the buildings to go round the back of the house and follow it over Rushton Hill to join the road at the corner by St James' church. Turn left and reach the car park in under 1.2 km (0.75 mile).

Historical Notes

Slaidburn: The Old Grammar School of 1717 stands close to the 15th century church of St Andrew at the south end of this very attractive village of stone. Inside the church are a Jacobean chancel screen of 1630 (unique in the county), Georgian box pews and a three-decker pulpit of the 1740s. In the centre of the village is the Hark to Bounty inn which used to house the manor court. Car park and toilets are available by the bridge.

Hammerton Hall: A residence of the local landed gentry of this name as early as the 13th century.

The Reservoir: Opened in 1932 to serve Blackpool, construction took ten years and involved an 8 km (5 miles) railway from Tosside and a village to house between 300 and 400 men and their families; both are now gone. The surface covers some 343 acres and its capacity is 2,640 million gallons. Three thousand acres of the catchment are planted with trees, most of which are conifers but there is a programme of introduction of broadleaved trees. Waymarked forest walks are available from the Gisburn Forest car park.

St James' church: Beneath the waters of the reservoir lies the hamlet of Stocks in Bowland. Its church was built in 1852 and this isolated little church replaced it in 1938 using some of the original stone. Inside you will find a brief history of Stocks.

Nature reserve and wildlife: Part of the shore and reservoir close to Gisburn Forest car park is designated a reserve (indicated on the information board) and has no access. The easiest place for a view is along the road towards St James' church; there is a private hide for Lancashire Trust for Nature Conservation members. The reservoir is a favourite haunt of a variety of waterfowl — wigeon, teal, tufted duck, pochard, goldeneye, goosander, Canada geese — and black-headed gulls breed on the island. Less familiar species are crossbills and great grey shrike in the forest in winter, and peregrines may be seen in the area on occasion. The more common species of moorland and grazing land can be expected on a walk in spring and summer.

Fairsnape Fells

Introduction: The south-western corner of the Bowland Fells stands out sharply when viewed from a wide area of the Fylde and the lowlands south of the Ribble. A large block of Access land makes them at least partially available to the walker and even this circumscribed ground can provide a significant challenge, especially in adverse weather and in the winter; a compass is essential. In this walk the fells are coupled with the magnificent embayment of Bleasdale and a circuit around the moorland edge.

Distance: Total distance is about 14.5 km (9 miles) which makes an easy day in good weather. Footpaths exist linking the start and Saddle End direct to Chipping which would add a further 5 km (3 miles). Maps — OS Landranger 102 & 103, OS Pathfinder 668 & 669.

Refreshments: Chipping village has a wide range of possibilities from an à la carte restaurant to pubs and a café, together with several village shops. There are toilets at the car park. Bleasdale post office has some refreshments available.

How to get there: The suggested start is from the bottom of the lane from Fell Foot (GR 602442) where there is roadside parking. Approach from Chipping village.

The Walk: Take the signed path on the western side of the lane and walk diagonally right across the field to contour round the steep slopes of Parlick Fell. Cross a tongue of

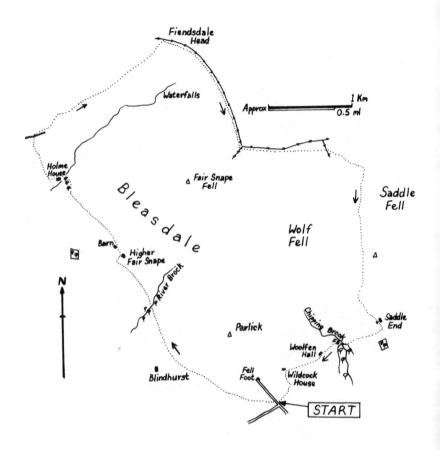

Fiendsdale
Head

Waterfalls

1 Km
Approx ————————
0.5 ml

Holme
House

B l e a s d a l e

△ Fair Snape
Fell

Saddle
Fell

Wolf
Fell

Barn

Higher
Fair Snape

River Brock

△

N

Parlick

△

Chipping Brook

Saddle
End

Woolfen
Hall

Blindhurst

Fell
Foot

Wildcock
House

START

Access land past two signs showing a map of it. At the second sign take the iron gate and stay inside the fell fence to follow an obvious track round to enter Bleasdale; Blindhurst farm is below on the left. Cross the rutted fell track at an angle and drop to a stile over the fence by a stream.

Walk right on the stony track and take the first gate on the left. Drop down to a group of trees and cross the infant river Brock, to follow the fence and track to Higher Fair Snape farm. Pass through the farm and emerge at '10 o'clock' via sheep pens by a barn. Immediately to your left is the small wood in which Bleasdale wooden circle lies hidden. The path is clear ahead to a shelterbelt of sycamores and swings round them to come past Holme House from the right; a place of swallows and sun between showers.

Commence the climb up the farm access track and turn right at the yellow arrow by the cattle grid. Follow the fell wall up direct (ignore the stile on the left) to join the path to Fiendsdale Head over the wall. You re-enter the Access Area here — even now the 'beware unexploded shells!' notice does have a relevance. The path climbs steadily. After rainy weather the waterfalls below Holme House Fell cut a white dash across the fell and there is a good view south to the Ribble Valley and Beacon Fell.

The vegetation gradually changes from bilberry and bracken to thin peat and heather, and at the Head the wet peat haggs give a feeling of isolation. Turn right, inside the fence, across deep eroded peat with heather moor opening out to the east on your left. The summit is reached at a cairn and pole (GR 597472) at about 520m (1,707 ft). A minor diversion south-west (244°) — a 1.6 km (1 mile) addition there and back — takes you to the trig point on top of Fair Snape Fell (GR 591468) and to Paddy's Pole and the view down into Bleasdale and out across the Fylde.

At the fence is a further notice on entry to Wolf Fell. Because this is an area covered by an Access Order and not an Access Agreement dogs are allowed (quite an impractical proposition by this stage!). Walk due east along the fence line with Pendle Hill ahead and Longridge Fell to your right to reach an up-and-over stile onto Saddle Fell and 'no dog land' again.

Drop down the fence line to a second stile and bear off at 125° to pick up a track which quickly descends the fell to a final Access notice and down to Saddle End farm. Take the stile to the right before the wood on the farm access road and bear back across the field to a broken stile in the right-hand corner. Walk ahead now to a footbridge over the Chipping Brook above a wood and climb the bank via a stile and gates to the left of Woolfen Hall. Through the farm buildings the right of way bears right up the field to the angle of the fell wall at Wildcock House and only then drops back down to the farm access track to rejoin the lane where you began. Perhaps only now will you notice the dilapidated sign which reads 'Bulls Grazing'.

Historical Notes

Access Areas: Fairsnape (648 acres), Saddle Fell (360 acres) and Wolf Fell (514 acres) are adjacent and make up one single block of Access land. The two former are subject to Access Agreements with the landowners, the latter was designated by an Access Order which explains why your dog is welcome on this aptly named section of the fell! Enter Wolf Fell direct by going up the lane from the start of the walk, past Fell Foot, on to Parlick and contour right below the top to a stile.

Bleasdale circle: This unusual circle, made of wooden posts not upright stones, lies just off the route but is hidden within a plantation (GR 572458) without direct public access.

Excavation revealed a double grave. The wooden posts are now marked by concrete pillars.

Chipping village and church: The village nestles in the broad valley between Longridge Fell and Parlick and deserves a little of your time. The name suggests Chipping was originally a market centre and its attractive stone houses still bring many visitors, especially at weekends; there are two car parks and toilets west of the church. Brabins School on Windy Street is dated 1683. St Bartholomew's church suffered Victorian restoration but the use of the site may date as early as AD 596. It became a separate parish from Whalley in 1041, had its tower added in 1450 and enjoyed earlier rebuilding in 1506. Despite all this it has, I feel, one of the pleasantest atmospheres for peaceful reflection.

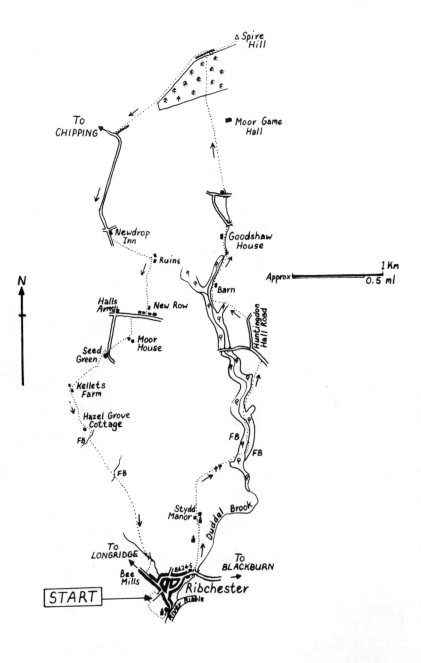

Ribchester and Longridge Fell

Introduction: The village of Ribchester is situated most delightfully beside the Ribble and is one of the most interesting places to visit in the whole of the county. Its Roman remains are the most extensive and it happens to be one of the very few places in the north of England the Roman name of which we can be sure of: Bremetennacum. The northern side of the valley at this point is formed by Longridge Fell which gives wide views at all seasons and is ablaze with heather in September. This walk links the two.

Distance: The walk itself takes a pleasant, if long, half day; 15 km (9.25 miles). If, however, you haven't visited Ribchester before you will surely want to take time to walk round the village and beside the river Ribble and to visit the Roman Museum and the Museum of Childhood and thus spend the whole day. Maps — OS Landranger 103, OS Pathfinder 669 & 680.

Refreshments: Ribchester has a wide range of refreshments available from cafe to pub, village shop to restaurant. You will also go directly past the Newdrop Inn (GR 644390) and within 100m of the Halls Arms (GR 644381).

How to get there: Ribchester is signed from miles around. The most convenient starting point is the car park behind the Roman Museum and church in Ribchester village; toilets are available (GR 649341).

The Walk: Leave the car park along the private road past the

43

tennis courts and take the footpath along the churchyard wall. The church itself is worth visiting and the museum is immediately beside it. Across the lane are seats beside the river and a view up valley towards Pendle Hill. A short detour along the river bank will take you to the site of the Roman baths.

Turn away from the river and up the street past the White Bull Hotel. Turn right at the main road and walk past the Ribchester Arms on the left. Use Stydd Lane left before the bridge and pass the parish centre and school on the right and the RC church of St Peter and St Paul on the left. Almost immediately you will come across one of Lancashire's most amazing treasures, the recently renovated almshouses and, within 100m on the right, the medieval Hospitaller church of St Saviour.

Go straight through the yard of the farm of Stydd Manor and follow the track due north across the field to a stile by the right-hand of two gates. Bear 65° to go left of a clump of large trees around a pond and edge slightly left across the field to enter the wood about 20m from the corner. Cross a footbridge over the Duddel Brook and turn left upstream past the ruins of a mill and pond (where combs were made from horn) to another footbridge. Cross back again and follow up the right-hand bank over a third footbridge, keeping up the bank over a bluff before dropping to cross once more to the left bank. Climb right to the woodland edge and enter the field and follow the wood boundary to a stile. Bear right now between two telegraph poles to exit onto Gallows Lane by the gate and walk left to the corner of Huntingdon Hall Road.

Turn right up the road and go left through a field gate on the bend 50m past the second house on the right (there is no sign here). Use the gate ahead and pass immediately in front of the caravan; notice the sign on the tree which reads 'From the little acorn grows the mighty oak'. At the field bear 284°

to the edge of the wood on the far side but turn right up its edge instead of entering it. Walk past the stone barn and drop to cross the brook for a final time before rising on a track past Goodshaw House to meet the road again. Use the road up to the turn right; on the way the first evidence of moorland vegetation appears.

Turn right and almost immediately left at the sign for 'Moor Game Hall Farm etc' and use the track straight on to where the metalling bears off right. Go ahead here and onto the heather moor; the view back is worth at least a glance now. The path is clear up the hill and through a plantation of Japanese larch and sitka spruce to meet a well worn cross track at the ridge. No one will mind you taking the permissive path right to the trig point on the top of Spire Hill and enjoying the fine view round from Chipping village below, clockwise past Ingleborough, Pendle Hill and the Anglezarke Moors.

Drop back to where you left the plantation and use the up-and-over stile to get to the far side of the wall before moving down it, through some rather wet patches and past grouse butts, to a road. Turn left along the verge and drop to the crossroads at the Newdrop Inn; there is a little alternative roadside parking here. Take the footpath left 20m past the inn and go diagonally right across the field to a stile and footbridge 20m up from the right-hand corner, then cross the next field to a gate by farm ruins. Stay on this side of the stream, walk south through a gateway and make for a stone stile onto a grassed lane in the right-hand corner. This reaches a road at New Row. Turn right to the end of the houses; the Halls Arms is 100m ahead.

Cross the road and follow the sign left towards Moor House but take the gate right just before the first barn. Follow the left-hand boundary to a stile onto Stoneygate Lane (crossing the line of a Roman road on the way) and turn left and immediately right into Seed Green. Go left round the buildings opposite a corrugated shed and walk down to the end of the green lane. Use the stile right and follow the hedge on the left. Aim for the gate between the new buildings at Kellets Farm and turn left on the access track. Use the stile to the left of Hazel Grove Cottage and hug the right-hand hedge to circle round and drop to a footbridge over a brook. Bear right and stay with the fence to the right-hand corner of the field, walking ahead to a stile by an oak tree. Cross the gully and move ahead again to cross a stream by a footbridge. Stay by the left-hand hedge and pass a silted pond bright with yellow flag in season. Ribchester church is now in sight with the woods of Osbaldeston on the far bank of the Ribble behind.

Follow a clear series of stiles down the fields to cross Boyce's Brook by a concrete bridge and emerge on the main road almost opposite Bee Mills on the edge of Ribchester. Turn left to go back to the car park.

Historical Notes

Ribchester: Despite having been a mill village making bobbins (one chimney and some other buildings remain on the Longridge road) Ribchester manages to feel mainly 17th and 18th century and a large number of visitors respond by crowding in, especially on summer weekends. The bridge over the Ribble, 1 km (0.8 mile) east of the village, dates from 1774 and the White Bull Hotel, in the village centre, is more than half a century earlier (1707) with a unique Tuscan-columned porch. St Wilfrid's church actually stands within the bounds of the Roman fort and is mainly 13th century with a 14th century tower; some of the stone used may well be Roman. The chantry chapel known as the Dutton Quire has an unusual roof construction.

Roman remains: The visible remains of Bremetennacum are

rather limited. In addition to the church taking up part of the site some of it has been washed away by the river. It was constructed by Governor Agricola in AD 79. The independent museum is in a special building beside the church and in the middle of the site of the fort. The best item is a helmet unearthed in 1796 (the original of which is in the British Museum). Opening times are afternoons 2–5pm March to October with longer opening from 11.30am to 5.30pm in July and August; the rest of the year Sunday 2–4pm only. There is an admission charge. Remains of the bath house are visible between the rear of the White Bull and the river. Walking there gives you the chance to say you have been on the long-distance Ribble Way!

Stydd (or Stidd): A tiny hamlet, and only just distinct from Ribchester, Stydd contains the rather plain St Peter and St Paul RC church and two of Lancashire's gems. St Saviour's is a small medieval church built by a Commandery of the Knights Hospitallers from Wakefield probably in the 1130s. The north doorway and windows are Norman and the south doorway Early English with a waterleaf motif on the capitals. There is also a Jacobean pulpit with canopy. The whole was restored in 1925. Just down the lane is an almshouse (1728) of five bays, the centre three of which have an arcade with Tuscan columns at first floor level which is reached by an open, curving staircase: quite brilliant.

Museum of Childhood: Attached to a toy shop on Church Street, Ribchester, and open except on Mondays. For anyone, of any age, who enjoys toys of all sorts and sizes this is an indulgence not to be missed. (Tel 025484-520.)

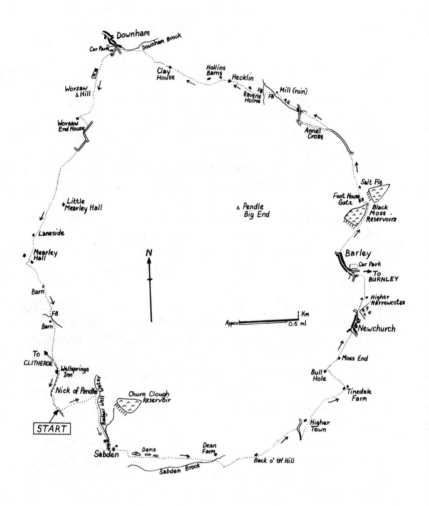

A Pendle Round

Introduction: From most of the Ribble Valley, and from the moor-tops north and south in the county, every view seems to have Pendle Hill in it. This isolated whale of a hill is not all that high (557m, 1,831 ft) but has dominated man around it since he first arrived, and continues to do so. One of the new districts had to be called Pendle and all except one transport route has to go round. Rather than go for the moorland plateau top, this walk takes a closer look at the sides of the hill that seems to be in their own back garden for half of Lancashire's folk, and discovers a variety of pretty villages, delightful churches, streams, woods and views.

Distance: A full day is needed for the 22.5 km (14 miles), especially if you want to stop and enjoy its full variety. Maps — OS Landranger 103, OS Pathfinder 669, 670, 680 & 681.

Refreshments: The route passes a variety of possibilities in Sabden, Newchurch, Barley and Downham from village shop to à la carte restaurant, and the Wellsprings Inn by the Nick of Pendle.

How to get there: I have chosen to start from the Nick of Pendle (GR 771385) simply because it has a grand view and gives a chance to stride out straight away; park in one of the old quarries. Approach from the A59 Clitheroe by-pass or follow signs for Sabden on the A671 or A6068 on the south. Many other start points are possible and I should select on the basis of your choice of refreshment.

The Walk: Turn towards Sabden and opposite the first gate on the right, turn left and join a track towards Churn Clough reservoir. Just before a gate turn right down the Badger Well Water and drop through a narrow field to enter Sabden village around the right-hand end of a terrace of cottages. Cross the bridge and bear right then left to pass St Nicholas' church on your right and, at the end of the lane, turn right along the hedge to a broken footbridge. Stride between the supports and turn up the broad valley of the Sabden Brook on a well used track past a series of old dams now full of horsetails and dabchicks.

Follow the track for a good 1½ km (1 mile) almost into the yard of Dean Farm and turn right between walls to enter Pendle District and what the map shows as 'The Forest of Pendle' at the bottom of Dean Height. Follow the path north-eastwards along the valley edge, first one side of the wall and then the other. At Back o' th' Hill the path diverts east round the garden. Continue ahead until you join Guide Lane at a corner. Here you can choose to go directly on the same line through Higher Town or to climb the lane right and pick up the Pendle Way to the left at the crest. The latter is the more interesting and gives a last view south over industrial east Lancashire and a view east towards the Yorkshire Dales.

Continue to follow the base of the slope to the empty buildings of Tinedale Farm and turn left across the valley almost to Bull Hole (where witch Demdike was accused of killing a sick cow). Pick up the path right with Newchurch in sight and pass through the garden at Moss End (where Jane and John Bulcock, two of those found guilty of witchcraft, lived) to enter the village by the school. Newchurch will surely delay you in a variety of ways. On leaving walk up the Barley road to the top of the brow and turn right on the track by a plantation. Pass the first building on the left and look carefully for the stile left into the field just before Higher

Harrowcotes farm. The path descends steeply to a track and a few minutes to the left will bring you to Barley village, a large car park and picnic site, toilets, information and refreshment.

Leave Barley along the Downham road but follow the track ahead for Black Moss at the signpost. Pass Lower Black Moss reservoir (completed in 1903) and turn left below the dam of the upper reservoir (1894). Bear right through the buildings of Foot House Gate to walk past Salt Pie on your right, to come to a fine view of the Big End of Pendle by a ford. A store of salt, delivered by packhorse from the Cheshire mines, used to be kept here. Keep right of the stream and join a metalled lane. At the cattle grid keep to the wall and drop to some cottages. The remains of Annel Cross lie on the moor to the left and now the Bowland Fells stand out ahead.

Go left over a stile past the cottages. Aim half right for trees in a steep clough and pass them on your left to reach a poor footbridge below a half-ruined small mill. Cross the stream, swing right round a barn, and cross the field to a wall gap and another poor footbridge. Climb up to the track to Ravens Holme but go left before the house and keep along the right-hand boundary; Penyghent stands out boldy to the north-east. The stile in the far right corner enables you to drop to Heklin farm where you need to pass the front of the buildings and go left of the large beech tree to leave barns on your right and find a stile out of the gully.

Pass Hollins farm and use the stile to the right past a gate (Downham Hall and Worsaw Hill are in clear view). Bear right of a gully to go between new buildings at Clay House and follow the outside of the right-hand boundary round to the bottom of the yard. Turn down the field to a stile and footbridge in the left-hand corner. A clear path crosses fields to enter Downham village by Downham Brook and its large population of ducks. If you do not already know it you will want to divert into the picturesque village; note that the post office closes on Wednesday afternoons!

Otherwise, bear left before the bridge. Ignore the first right to car park and toilets but go straight ahead at the corner on the track between cottages. Keep to the right-hand boundaries past a wood and along the bottom of Worsaw Hill, a limestone reef knoll which grows lusher, juicier grass and roses everywhere in season. Just before Worsaw End House a gate below a small cliff takes you left down to the access track and up to the road. Go right and round left and right bends to a footpath sign for Mearley. A footbridge and path takes you through to a surfaced lane. The views west across the valley to Longridge Fell, Beacon Fell and Parlick are fine.

Follow the track ahead past Little Mearley Hall on the left (with fine bay windows and a porch which came from Sawley Abbey) and a glimpse of Clitheroe Castle on your right. Pass Lane Side to join a metalled surface to reach Mearley Hall, with stone knobs on its field gateway! Continue past the buildings on the left and turn left on the first track. Use the stile and start to climb heading for the left of the barn on the brow. Aim for the just visible roof of a second barn. Preston and even Southport are visible towards the sea. Drop down to cross Howcroft Brook at a footbridge. Follow the fell wall up and round through lapwing country and at the corner head straight to the road up from Pendleton and Clitheroe. Walk left up the verge past the Wellsprings Inn to the Nick of Pendle.

Historical Notes

The villages: Each of the villages around Pendle has its own character and the four· on the route are quite distinctive. **Sabden** is a plain and no nonsense sort of place which only became a separate parish from Newchurch in 1841.

Newchurch in Pendle is airy and open with an eye to the tourist potential of the witches. **Barley** nestles its stones down below the Big End of Pendle and caters well for the passerby. The name probably derives from the infertility of the land in earlier times, but in the 13th century extensive cattle ranching was carried on. **Downham** is a medieval village which remains all-of-a-piece as an estate village rebuilt by the Asshetons and really needs to make no great effort to look pretty against the backdrop of the hill.

Churches: Two of the churches on our route are worth stopping off to see. St Mary's, at Newchurch, is a delightful building in Georgian style (1740) with an earlier tower (1544) on the site of a chapel of ease of 1250. A pleasing interior with an 'eye of God' in the wall of the tower and a sundial dated 1718 on the south-west corner of the nave. The so-called 'witches grave' is of the wrong date. St Leonard's at Downham is mostly a rebuilding of the 20th century and shows what can be done with careful control. The best view of the village and Pendle is from by the church.

The Pendle Witches: The witch trials of 1612 have entered national folklore. Retelling the tale here is impractical but several small volumes available locally tell it more or less as it really was; ten people were hanged. Robert Neill's novel 'Mist over Pendle' is a fine example of what human imagination can do with the story but it's really Pendle Hill itself which dominates again. Even though the accused made no mention of Pendle at their trial they clearly *ought* to have done and the locals have been cashing in on that thought for a good many years now. Roughlee Hall, where the best known, Alice Nutter, is said to have lived, actually lies about 3 km (2 miles) east of Barley on the Barrowford road.

Pendle Heritage Centre: If you have transport and time, a visit to the centre in Barrowford is well worth the effort. It occupies the farmhouse of Park Hill, dating from the 17th century, at the junction of the A682 and B6247 (GR 683398) and illustrates the life of this area through the years. The Information Centre is open daily all year but the exhibition is only open afternoons daily (2.00 to 4.30pm) between Easter and the last Sunday in November bar Mondays (Bank Holidays excepted). Tea room, picnic site and toilets available.

Pendle Way and local map: A 72 km (45 miles) route circuits the District of Pendle. This walk uses part of it from Higher Town to Barley. Copies of a pack of guide maps with information are available from Pendle Heritage Centre and other Information Centres in the area. A superior walking map on a large scale called 'Paths Around Pendle' giving footpath, and much other, information is also available locally.

Geology: A fairly obvious question is 'Why does Pendle stand out so much?' The detailed answer is complex but is associated with mountain-building movements which resulted in a series of west/south-westerly trending folds of the rocks in the region of what is now Ribblesdale. Pendle itself is topped by the relatively hard millstone grit rock which dips away steeply at over 40° under the Sabden valley.

Round the other side of Pendle the more or less isolated lumps of limestone, of which Worsaw Hill is one, are made of fossil-rich reefs which stood up above the sea bed at the time of their formation. The muddy materials, which came to form shales, in the hollows between them are much softer and have eroded away to leave the reefs standing up once more as the knolls we see today.

Beacon Fell
and The River Brock

Introduction: Beacon Hill was one of the first Country Parks, created in 1970. The top, at 873 ft, is open moor where bilberries grow profusely. As this pleasant walk rambles across the fell and along the valley of the river Brock, butterflies, wild flowers, birds and other wildlife make the circuit a delight.

Distance: The circuit suggested, of 8.5 km (5.3 miles), provides an easy half day. Maps — OS Landranger 102, OS Pathfinder 668.

Refreshments: The nearest avilable refreshments are at Bleasdale and Whitechapel post offices, and the pub in Inglewhite.

How to get there: I suggest starting at the Fell House car park on Beacon Fell where there are toilets and an information kiosk. Beacon Fell is well signed from the A6 and B5269 north of Preston (GR 565426).

The Walk: Have a word with one of the friendly Rangers at the kiosk before leaving the car park and get an update on any local items of interest and, perhaps, the weather. Pass the toilet block and take the path through the spruce plantation to cross the circuit road at the first bend. Drop steeply straight ahead across the field to a gap between woods and reach a lane. Turn right and immediately left

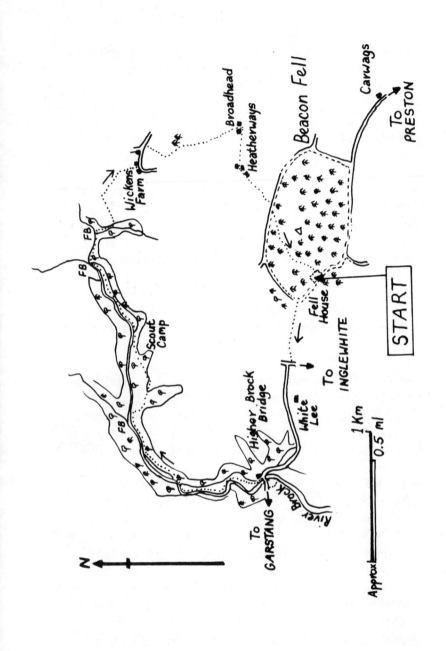

along White Lee Lane to descend to Higher Brock Bridge. Here there is a picnic site and car park and the start of a downstream trail, which you could add to your walk if you wish.

Take the path on the right-hand bank of the river before the bridge and walk upstream. The first 1½ km (1 mile) is through fields and you then enter woodland. All around is a mass of flower colour in season accompanied by butterflies (orange tips were common when I last passed), and followed by the fruit of wild raspberry and blackberry. If need be, you can cut back to the start from the ford and footbridge at Snape Rake Lane (GR 553442).

The next section has a permissive path through the aptly named Boggy Wood — it is very boggy and clarty with clay! Alternatively, turn right up the lane to a path on the left at the top of the wood and descend back to the river through Waddecar Scout Camp with many bird and bat boxes affixed to trees. You soon enter fields again with a plantation of larch and spruce on the right.

At the 'Weak bridge' sign turn up the right-hand valley and right again over a footbridge across the next side stream to climb an old track to the top of the wood. Beacon Fell and the Bleasdale Fells are now in view. Walk half left along an old hedge line to a gate and stile and turn half right along a fence on your left to a yellow arrow which directs you to the road at Wickens farm, dated 1850. Go left to a house at the road junction.

A gap in the wall on the right is the start of a path up the field to a stile. Bear left to two large trees and walk right along the fence line to the farm at Broadhead. Go between the buildings and right on the track to the next farm of Heatherways. Follow the signs through the complex of old and new buildings and head directly up towards Beacon Fell just above you. Cross the circuit road and turn up diagonally right through spruces. When you emerge from the plantation angle right across the fell top and down an old wall line back to Fell House.

Historical Notes

Beacon Fell Country Park: Until 1909 the fell was grazed land of the farm at Fell House. It was then bought by the former Fulwood UDC (Preston) as water gathering ground and was planted with about 115 acres of sitka spruce, larch and Scots pine. Fifty years later it had become surplus to needs and the plantations deteriorated until they were acquired by Lancashire CC and turned into one of the first Country Parks in 1970. The top is at 266 m (873 ft) and is capped by hard millstone grit resulting in open moor on which bilberries grow profusely; the trig point has an indicator. Despite the high number of visitors, wildlife always seems to be abundant — indicating the great success of management by the Ranger Service.

Trail along the river Brock: The trail, marked by numbered posts, runs about 2.5 km (1.5 miles) from the car park at Lower Brock Mill (GR 549431) downstream to the derelict mill at Brock Bottom (GR 544421). Leaflets are available from the Lancashire Trust for Nature Conservation, Cuerden Park Wildlife Centre, Shady Lane, Bamber Bridge, Preston PR5 6AU. Tel 0772-324129.

White Lee Lane: The more or less straight section of the lane is a good example of the sequence of change, from a route along which cattle were moved — resulting in it being surprisingly wide between the hedge lines — to a cart track, which is when it was probably first ditched, to a tarmac road for cars much marrower than it needs to be. White Lee Hall has been recently rebuilt to its original Jacobean plan.

The Marshes of Asland

Introduction: A considerable proportion of lowland Lancashire has been reclaimed from marsh or sea. The main river which drains much of the area south of the Ribble used to be known as the river Asland in its lower reaches but is now more often called the Douglas throughout its length; the map still retains both names. This walk gives an opportunity to fill your horizons with sky for a change. It begins near Tarleton lock on the Rufford branch of the Leeds and Liverpool canal, and the first half of the walk follows embankments beside the river and then the marshes which border the river Ribble. It is a fascinating insight into the problems and results of land reclamation and water transport, in a peaceful and beautiful setting.

Distance: A good half day, easy walk of 13 km (8 miles). Maps — OS Landranger 102, OS Pathfinder 688.

Refreshments: The Dolphin Inn (often unbiologically called 'The Fish') is about halfway round the route (GR 458254) and the Black Horse and Rose and Crown are more or less opposite each other at the southern end of Much Hoole (approx GR 465224).

How to get there: The suggested starting point is at the start of the old section of the A59 just north of the roundabout at the junction with the B5247 (GR 462216).

The Walk: Where the main road crosses a drain is a path due west which joins the embankment of the river Asland in

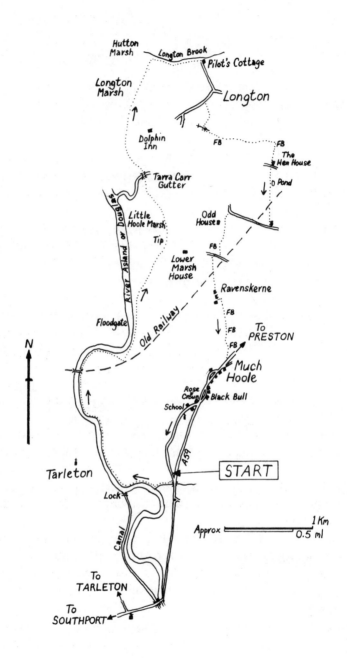

Hutton
Marsh

Longton Brook

Pilot's Cottage

Longton
Marsh

Longton

Dolphin
Inn

FB

FB

The
Hen House

Tarra Carr
Gutter

Pond

Odd
House

Little
Hoole Marsh

Tip

FB

Lower
Marsh
House

Ravenskerne

FB

Floodgate

FB

To
PRESTON

FB

Much
Hoole

Rose
Crown

Black Bull

School

Tarleton

START

A59

Lock

Canal

N

To
TARLETON

To
SOUTHPORT

Approx

1 Km
0.5 ml

250m. Follow this right, past Tarleton lock at the end of the Rufford Branch Canal with the village above. The rich silt land on your right carries amazing crops of things like cabbage, cauliflower and barley and the tidal river and lock have a crop of pleasure craft and the occasional real fishing boat still. Sand martins swoop for flies in the summer over the water and cattle graze the strip between the river and the houses of Tarleton. Continue past the old railway bridge over the river and bend round right and left to the floodgate at GR 457233.

The path now leaves the riverside and follows the inner edge of the salt marsh; oystercatcher and shelduck nest here. Ahead is the man-made mound of a county council tip. Keep right of this and rejoin the embankment beyond the newly grassed area and cross Tarra Carr Gutter. Pick up the embankment on the far side to join the Ribble Way at GR 456254, at the lane end by the Dolphin Inn. Walk ahead until the Ribble Way turns right and follow the signs. At the turn Warton Airfield and Freckleton are to the left across the Ribble, Fairsnape Fell is ahead over Ashton-on-Ribble, and round to the east, Darwen Tower stands out on the edge of the Anglezarke Moors.

Follow right up the Longton Brook to a pair of old stone bridges and sheep folds and use the stile and footbridge on the right. Follow the edge of the fields to exit on a metalled lane at Pilot's Cottage. Walk right to a road junction and turn right again and pick up the footpath 20m beyond the white house on the left.

Aim for the radio mast ahead to the corner of the field and then turn on a bearing of 212° to cross to a ditch and fence and walk to the stile and footbridge in the corner on the left. Follow the signs along an old hedge line (this is the only field in Lancashire in which I have met a bull in recent years; his age wasn't too apparent and I didn't enquire closely! The far side of a broad dyke provides a handy alternative if

61

required). After passing through a horse paddock turn right at a wet patch before an overgrown lane and cross an exceedingly decrepit footbridge to pass between a fence and hedge to meet Hall Lane beside 'The Hen House'. Cross to the sign for Hall Carr Lane and pass a pond to the left, full of yellow flag. Cross the old railway line again and walk the length of a narrow field to the lane. Turn right.

Go past the railway bridge abutments and turn left on the path at the bend by Odd House. The path is the sunken track by the hedge of cherries and sloes to the left of the house. At the bridge and stile bear left along the edge of the market garden to a track and join the lane. Fifty metres to the right take the footpath left and cross to a concrete-fenced kissing gate over the railway once more. Aim to the breeze block wall visible across the field and pass left of the buildings between hedge and fence to a lane. Turn left and immediately right along the ditch at the bottom of a garden. Cross two narrow fields and at the third footbridge follow the right-hand hedges and fence to the main A59. Turn right to the Rose and Crown (the Black Bull on your left) and use the old road past the school and church to return to the start.

Historical Notes

The Canal: There is a very obvious marina on the far side of the river just after the start of the walk. This is at the lock at the Tarleton end of the Rufford Branch of the Leeds and Liverpool Canal. The lock can only be entered at high tide. The river (Asland or Douglas, as you prefer) was made navigable from the estuary to Wigan as early as 1742 as a way of transporting coal. The branch canal was built as far as Sollom in 1781 and was extended in 1805. The river was diverted and the canal uses the old river bed between Sollom and Bank Bridge. There are eight locks in 7 miles. In the middle 1800s slate, iron ore and gunpowder were imported through Tarleton.

Land reclamation: The first half of the walk follows obvious embankments beside the river and then the marshes which border the river Ribble. An immediate first assumption is that what prompted the massive effort needed to build them was the attraction of the reclaimed agricultural land; not so however. The real attraction here was to find a way of keeping the Ribble channel free for shipping going up river to the port of Preston, which operated between 1806 and 1981. The various Ribble Navigation Companies, and then Preston Corporation, carried out the majority of this work during the latter half of the 19th century. Improvement of navigation of the river Asland also resulted in major changes and its outlet was moved from approximately the position of the Dolphin Inn to much closer to Tarleton. Early work on the embankments (or 'training walls', as they were called) took place in the region of Banks, near Southport, around 1810 and the Hesketh Banks, west of the river Asland were built between 1859 and 1883. Hutton Marsh was partially enclosed in the mid 1880s and a further embankment was made to the west (on Longton Marsh) in 1898. The elements proved too much for this, however, and it was breached by storms in 1907, 1925 and 1927 and never remade thereafter. A close look at the local OS map will show that parts of it still remain way out on the marsh. The whole series of operations, south and north of the Ribble, were, in any case, only partially successful and the channel had to be regularly dredged throughout the time of its use.

St Mary's chapel: On the skyline, looking beyond Tarleton Lock, is St Mary's chapel beside the main A59. The main brick structure was built in 1719 and the stone-topped tower with an open rotunda added in 1824. Well worth the short diversion along the road from the start point.

St Michael's church, Much Hoole: The main part is brick, of

63

1628, with attractive windows and the porch is of the same date. The tower was added in 1722 with contrasting stone facing. The font is dated 1663, the pulpit 1695. The inside is simple with box pews. When curate here, in 1629, Jeremiah Horrocks was the first person to observe the passage of the planet Venus across the face of the sun and so helped to show that the planets rotate around the sun and not the earth. The observation site was Carr House (1613), just on the Bretherton side of the roundabout by the start point.

Anglezarke Moor

Introduction: To the east of Chorley, Anglezarke Moor is a great dome of grass moorland, breaking the incoming south-westerly winds off the sea. It lies just to the north of Winter Hill, so readily identified by its TV mast, and for many, even temporary, exiles these West Pennine moorlands announce arrival home. They typify man's long history in the Pennines and have a unique natural history too. Quarries and lead mines, Bronze Age burial sites and 19th century reservoirs are some of the points of interest on this fascinating walk, which also visits the attractive villages of Rivington and White Coppice. Rivington Hall is 17th century, while its 100 ft barn and Great House Barn are outstanding cruck built structures. White Coppice was originally an industrial settlement, but nowadays its stone cottages and cricket ground with the moors beyond form an attractive and peaceful picture.

Distance: The circuit will take a full day and is 18.75 km (11.6 miles). Maps — OS Landranger 109, OS Pathfinder 700.

Refreshments: Snack refreshments are available at Great Barn Information Centre (GR 628138) and more substantial food will be found at Rivington Barn at weekends (GR 633144). Tea rooms are open less frequently in Rivington village (GR 627145).

How to get there: The West Pennine Moors Recreation Area is signed from the M61, Junction 6 (signed for Horwich). Follow the A6 or the A673 north-west for Horwich and take

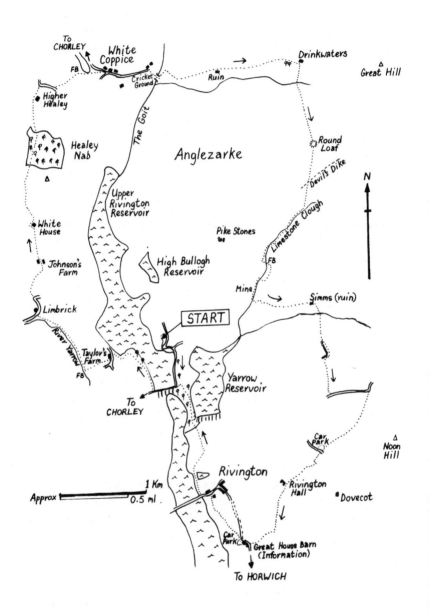

the turn signed for Rivington, then follow the sign for White Coppice to a car park by the old Leicester Mill quarry at GR 620160.

The Walk: Walk out of the car park along Moor and Knowsley Lanes with the reservoir on your right and cross the dam which gives a good view back to the Anglezarke Quarry above the car park and Healey Nab half-left. The quarry is now famous with climbers and was the source of countless stone setts for road paving throughout the 19th century. Turn right on the footpath past some sweet chestnuts and follow the reservoir bank north to a new section of retaining wall. Exit onto a lane at Taylor's farm (dated 1719). Go left and immediately right along a bridleway overhung with branches and down to the river Yarrow.

Cross neither footbridge nor ford but stay on the right-hand bank and follow the river downstream through alders and ash to a lane at Limbrick close by a motorway bridge. Walk up the lane to a right-angle bend and ahead on a 'Private Road'. Go behind Johnson's farm to a stile and a path up to a small wood and pond. There is a good view back now to Rivington Pike and Winter Hill. Cross the field beyond the wood to the left hand of White House buildings and turn right. Take the left-hand track to contour round Healey Nab with Chorley below to the left. The path goes between two widely-spaced hedges with heather moor and a plantation of Scots pine on the right. There is a fine view back to Ashurst Beacon and Parbold Hill. Enter a wood and take the upper path past some western hemlocks. Ignore side paths and take the old track down a field past Higher Healey and turn right at the lane.

In 200m take the footpath on the left with the view opening up ahead to the moor and Great Hill. Go diagonally right and cross a footbridge at the top end of a small reservoir to reach

White Coppice by a picnic table and seat. Cross a stone bridge and walk up Coppice Lane past the cottages and fine gardens to the most un-flat and unusual cricket ground in Lancashire. Clear signs say 'No Football' but alternative car parking, at least, is available here.

Pass the club house and cross the bridge over the Goit, which brings water from the Roddlesworth reservoirs, to enter the Access Area. Take the path which climbs to the left past the old Ramblers' Association sign (which was erected from the Thomas Rickerby Memorial Fund, it says). At the first ruins turn and look back down on Healey Nab and Chorley. You climb steadily to meet a path coming up from Brinscall and go right by an isolated beech wood and new plantings to the ruined farm at Drinkwaters where there is a memorial seat and a well.

The tumulus of Round Loaf and the mast on Winter Hill are visible due south across grass and heather moor. Drop to, and cross, the stream above a waterfall and rise again to Round Loaf. The view from here, on a fine day, extends round through the Peckforton Hills, to Wales, and to the southern Lakes and the Bowland Fells. Use the path heading just west of south towards the reservoir to cross Devil's Dike and strike the upper reaches of Limestone Clough. Pick up a path which joins a track at the top of some relatively recent plantations (a bearing of 302° will take you on a short diversion across the moor to Pike Stones long barrow). Cross a footbridge and stile to continue on the opposite side of the clough and use two more up-and-over stiles to eventually drop in to the clough and cross the stream to look at the remains of the lead mines. Go down stream to the concrete bridge and cross back to zig-zag up and bear east into the upper Yarrow Valley.

At the ruin of Simms (GR 637165) drop south to cross the river. Follow ahead at the sign through a very boggy patch and pick up a line of arrowed posts. At the second post follow the wall on the right and turn left at the wall end at the fingerpost, with Rivington dovecot in sight. At the lane turn up left to a right-angled bend and pick up the path to the right along the fell bottom.

Follow through to a car park below the dovecot and go ahead at the entrance on an up-and-over stile. At the third stile go left and right on a track which follows the stream down to Rivington Hall Barn. Walk round left through the strutting peacocks and leave the main drive to your right. At the junction of tracks turn right and bear left on a path through the wood which exits beside Great House Barn Information Centre.

Leave the centre by a path through Great House Arboretum at the entrance, to drop to a track which meets the village road beside the school (1905). Cross the road and turn right at the dam along a bridleway. After crossing an arm of the reservoir climb and bear left along an unsurfaced track towards the embankment of Yarrow Reservoir. Almost at the top bear left down a stony track to exit on to Knowsley Lane and walk right, back to the start.

Historical Notes

West Pennine Moors Recreation Area: Between Chorley and Haslingden, and Blackburn and Bolton lie more than 230 square km (90 square miles) of moorland, valley and reservoir. Since the mid 1970s Lancashire CC, North West Water, and the various District and Metropolitan Councils have jointly managed a Recreation Plan for the area and operate Ranger and Information Services. Access Areas have been created on both Winter Hill and the Anglezarke Moors. The Anglezarke Woodland Trail starts from the start point of this walk and the Upper Rivington Reservoir Trail from Rivington village.

Reservoirs: There are eight reservoirs in this immediate area holding about 3,950 million gallons covering over 10,000 acres. Most were built over a period between 1847 and 1857 with several of them interconnected. Upper Roddlesworth and Yarrow were added later. The massive embankments are built of earth with a puddled clay core and pitched with stone on the inside to prevent erosion by wave action. Water is provided to a large area including Liverpool, St Helens and Wigan and it can also be fed into Manchester supplies.

Lead Mining: Mining in Lead Mines Clough dates from 1692. They quickly made a profit and Margaret, the widow of Sir Richard Standish, seems to have attempted to corner this entirely for herself, even going to the extent of destroying the equipment and diverting a stream into the mines! They were worked until 1789 with some success but were then abandoned until a further attempt to open them was made between 1829 and 1837, but without new reserves of ore being found. An explanatory leaflet is available from the Information Centres and the Slime Pit, Water Wheel Pit, and a drainage sough are visible in the valley. The washed, lead-rich material was sold off for smelting elsewhere. In addition to lead the mine also produced a barium mineral called witherite (named after a Birmingham chemist) which, though poisonous, was used in medicines and in the manufacture of porcelain.

Round Loaf and prehistoric remains: This large mound has not been excavated so what it really is remains something of a mystery and the marking of 'tumulus' on the map is no more than wishful thinking. Noon Hill, above the dovecot car park, has a cairn which has been excavated and burials, arrowheads and a Bronze Age food vessel were uncovered. On the moor, north-west of Lead Mines Clough (GR 627171) is a chambered cairn known as Pikestones. Dated between 3000 and 2000 BC it was robbed of its contents long ago. The Devil's Dike, met above Lead Mines Clough, is a long, shallow trench which may be an earthwork but it has also been suggested could have been part of the boundary of a medieval deer park.

Rivington: Rivington village, around its sloping green, is an attractive and deservedly popular spot. The church dates originally from the mid 1500s but was rebuilt in the 1660s; it is aisleless. There is also a Unitarian church, founded as early as 1662, but this building is 1703. The stone houses are much of a style, whatever age they actually are individually. Even the more recent of the school (founded 1566) buildings, of 1905, fit in.

Rivington Hall Barn (beside the Hall and open on Sundays only), which is over 30m long (100 ft), and Great House Barn (the Information Centre and tea room) are outstanding cruck-built structures well renovated. The basic structure in each case dates from soon after 1700 (though different informants give different dates!) but the technique is very much older and the sites may have been used for agricultural purposes for a thousand years before. Both are Grade 1 listed buildings. Rivington Hall itself dates from the late 1690s with a five-bay brick facade of 1744.

White Coppice: Originally an industrial hamlet, known as Warth, White Coppice on a summer weekend attracts many. At any time of the year the combination of stone cottages, the series of lodges, the trees and the cricket ground with the moor beyond forms a picture quite at variance with an industrial past of bleach and dye works and a cotton mill, which did not close until 1914.

Farming on Anglezarke: The word 'Anglezarke' probably derives from a Norse personal name and a word in Old Norse

71

indicating summer grazing so there can be little doubt that, in common with much of the hill land of Lancashire, farming has gone on here over a long period. Analysis of the pollen found in the peat shows that man had significantly cleared the Lancashire hills of tree cover before 1000 BC. The subsequent wetter climate led to peat formation over the flatter ground and gentler slopes. Grazing then prevented any re-establishment of trees where they might otherwise have grown.

It comes as a surprise today to find the ruins of farms like Drinkwaters (and the even higher Great Hill farm) so high on the hills. The few operational farms left are generally much lower down and use the moors for sheep grazing and, sometimes, a few cattle. The improved fields around the old farms still show green against the browner moor and not only richer grazing was provided but crops of hay and oats too. The maximum extent of farming in the hills was probably during the Napoleonic Wars, when England had to be self-sufficient, and before the flood tide of the industrial revolution drew people to the towns. Town worthies subsequently bought up moorlands and dammed their valleys to supply increasing water needs.

Wycoller and The Brontë Way

Introduction: Anyone who knew Wycoller in the decades after the Second World War will have known a slowly decaying piece of Pennine history which had a touch of the picturesque, and even a little romance but which epitomised a disdain for our heritage which could be felt by the most thick skinned. Equally, the present conservation area shows what is possible with care and imagination. This former weaving hamlet has been reconstructed and now incorporates craft and information centres. It also includes one of the finest clapper bridges in England. Ruined Wycoller Hall is thought to have been the model for Ferndean Manor in Charlotte Brontë's 'Jane Eyre', and the Brontë connection is enhanced on this walk by following part of the Brontë Way which runs from Wycoller to Haworth. The surrounding moors are filled with wildlife and there are fine views along the route.

Distance: The circuit is a gentle day of 13 km (8 miles) but you will, surely, want to spend some time looking closely at Wycoller as well. Maps — OS Landranger 103, OS Pathfinder 681, 701.

Refreshments: The Craft Centre in Wycoller serves excellent snacks and light meals. There is also Herder's Arms on the Colne to Keighley road.

How to get there: Leave the A6068 Keighley road in Colne on

73

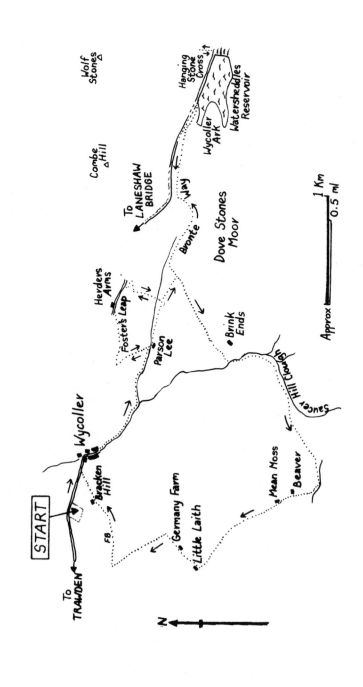

the B6250 for Trawden; a sharp, steep, left turn is signed for Wycoller. The most convenient place to park is at the Lancs CC car park about 0.25 km (250 yards) short of the hamlet (GR 926394).

The Walk: Walk down the footpath beside the lane to enter Wycoller at its northern end. Most who have not visited before will want to spend some time here, probably with the help of one of the guidebooks available from the Craft Centre. The now largely refurbished collection of buildings will impress even those uninterested in architecture. When open, also view the displays in the Countryside Centre. Beside this are toilets (including disabled) and a picnic site on the edge of a small lodge.

Leave along the track on the nearside of the beck, overhung with alder, sycamore and hawthorn and with a series of small falls. Follow the Pendle/Brontë Way signs to Parson Lee. A short side trip across the beck and up the valley side brings you to the massive stones of Foster's Leap where, it is said, a member of the Cunliffe family of Wycoller jumped the considerable gap between them. Return to Parson Lee and carry on up the valley on the unmade road.

The view opens out now and Dove Stones Moor rises to the right and Combe Hill to the left beyond the field boundaries. Across, on the left-hand skyline stands the Herder's Arms on the Colne to Keighley road and the path via Foster's Leap and another back to this point via the houses in the old quarry — known as Higher Key Stiles — make it possible to include a pub lunch if you wish.

At the T-junction of tracks at the top of the brow choose whether to include the spur route to Watersheddles and back.

Assuming you elect for this, turn left on the track signed Brontë Way and make your way up to the head of the valley following the signs for the 'Concessionary Route'. Just before you reach the nearest point to the road your feet will cross the watershed between the Irish Sea and the North Sea and the valve tower of Watersheddles Reservoir will be just in sight. For the fun of it, it is worth continuing for ten minutes to just beyond the dam where you meet the boundary of Yorkshire (the Oakworth area of Bradford) and look down the brackened valley of the upper river Worth. Only 50 metres onto the moor from the boundary sign on the road are the remains of Hanging Stone Cross, one of the many which marked the ways across these hills in the past. Sadly much of their length is closed to us and the rocks of Wolf Stones on the northern skyline are inaccessible from the Lancashire side. Return the way you came, the up-valley view creating a totally new impression, and drop back to pick up the Pendle Way once more.

Shortly beyond the junction with the track you came up from Parson Lee is a sign bearing you to the right off the track and onto an old bridleway which cuts across the top of Deep Clough and then descends to a ford below the isolated farm of Brink Ends. The route now ascends Saucer Hill Clough with the mass of Boulsworth Hill, the upper slopes covered in peat haggs, on your left. Underfoot, the track still has paving in many places from packhorse days. On the right is a massive well made, and very black, gritstone wall marking the edge of farmed land. Over the brow, drop to a stream where the map marks a ford which is no longer there, and take the stile into the field on the right (GR 929370).

Cross to the next wall and then climb diagonally right to Beaver farm and go round it via the up-and-over stiles and left down a field to Mean Moss. Here, take the wicket gate by the garage and walk immediately in front of the house to stiles leading straight ahead towards Little Laith. Turn right before the next stile, walk the 200m to Germany farm and pass it left to join the track. In a further 200m there is a crossing of tracks where you turn left and downhill. Even on the poorest of days you will already have seen the bulk of Pendle Hill rising across the valley and slightly to the left. The next ⅓ mile gives a chance for a last savouring of the view until you reach the remains of the first stone wall on the left. Turn right over a stile, walk diagonally across the field to a gate (GR 924391) and follow the boundary line on the right to cross a stream by a footbridge. A few paces diagonally to the left will bring you in sight of Bracken Hill. Go in front of the house and follow the marker arrows down to Wycoller again.

Historical Notes

Wycoller: Detailed guides to the buildings of the former weaving hamlet and its surroundings are available at the Information and Craft Centres: the full investigation they deserve is beyond our scope here. The remains of Wycoller Hall are basically those of a remodelling of a former farmhouse (1550) by Henry Owen Cunliffe in the 1770s. By all accounts he was a typical sporting English squire who lived well beyond his means. The ruined house is thought to have been the inspiration for Ferndean Manor in Charlotte Brontë's 'Jane Eyre'. Along the river is a fine series of old bridges (including a clapper bridge which rivals that at Postbridge, in Devon, as England's finest), fords and stepping stones — sufficient of 'nemselves to make a visit worthwhile.

Behind Wycoller Hall is Tenter Field (where cloth was stretched on frames to bleach in the sun). Part of the field boundary is formed from massive, split stones. These mark the existence of 'vaccaries', or medieval cattle ranches, set up by the lords of the manor here in the Forest of Trawden, in Pendle Forest and in Rossendale in the late 1200s. Wycoller probably derives its name from Old English 'wic', meaning a dairy farm.

Reservoirs: At Watersheddles the walk reaches the first of a series of reservoirs constructed by the Borough of Keighley in the 1870s. Construction continued on the Yorkshire side well into the 20th century (Lower Laithe 1920). The relative collapse of industrial demand for more water in the North-West and Yorkshire in general since the Second World War, coupled with a steadily increasing awareness of the recreational value of the countryside at large has produced a new perspective. Although bought for a reservoir, the Wycoller Valley was never flooded and such use would be unthinkable today. Much of the hill land remains water gathering ground, however, and public access is surely more limited than it need be.

The Brontë Way: The route runs from Wycoller to Haworth (14 km, 9 miles). It is important to remember that the central, concessionary, section may be closed on occasion because of fire risk or grouse shooting. A check can be made by telephoning Haworth 42329 or Colne 861286.

Bird life of the moors: The moors and fields around Wycoller seem particularly rich in bird life though the species are common throughout the moorland of the county.

Perhaps the two most characteristic birds of the moors are the red grouse and the curlew. The former feeds only on young heather shoots and so its numbers are linked to management of the moors by burning. In recent years good management has become less common and EEC agricultural policies have encouraged overstocking with sheep; both lead to loss of heather moor. The curlew is common on the grass moors and the rushy upper fields, often accompanied by redshank. The small stream valleys are home to ring ouzels, grey wagtails and dippers, and the common sandpiper haunts the reservoir margins. Many of the reservoirs are home to flocks of Canada geese which readily breed. Skylark and meadow pipit sing loud above the grasslands in spring and early summer. Wheatears perch and 'tick' with annoyance at your passing from a rock or wall.

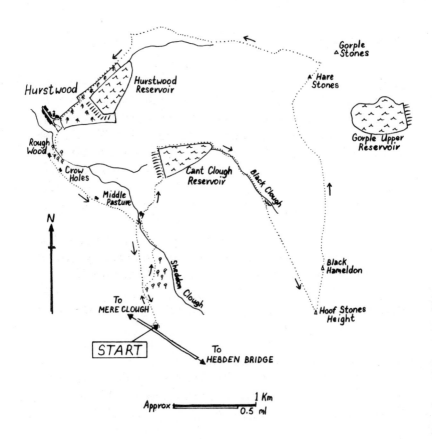

Hoof Stones Height and The Gorple Stones

Introduction: A massive sweep of moorland lies along the Lancashire–Yorkshire border in the South Pennine area. A large part of it was closed to walkers until relatively recently, and some still is. East of Burnley lies the large Worsthorne Moor Access Area and this walk makes use of the freedom to roam that this gives. Crossing the open moor makes carrying a compass and a knowledge of how to use it essential; weather conditions may change unpredictably.

Distance: In good weather this makes an easy day of 15 km (9.4 miles); bad weather makes it a hard day at any time of year. Maps — OS Landranger 103, OS Pathfinder 681.

Refreshments: A delightful tea room will be found in Hurstwood.

How to get there: Approach from the A646 through Mere Clough from the Burnley direction or up the bank from Pudsey west of Todmorden. Start from the North West Water car park on Long Causeway (GR 892289).

The Walk: Use the surfaced path to descend towards Sheddon Clough. At the fork take the right-hand path between the walls and down amongst the old workings. Bear left across the stream and turn right up the bank just before the wall on the left ends at two oak trees.

As you emerge from the clough turn right on the track and

aim for the Cant Clough Reservoir dam. On a bright April morning the air here was full of larks and drumming snipe and a flock of linnets swept across a small patch of burnt moor grass. At the dam a pair of the ubiquitous Canada geese honked noisily at my passing.

Across the dam follow the track up the reservoir to the inlet and exit through the wall onto the open moor. A marked path leads left of the stream up to the Gorple Stones. Be more adventurous, however, and take advantage of the access agreement and follow the right-hand branch of the stream up Black Clough. This narrows after a while and even the sheep trods cross and recross the stream. The small cliff marked on the map (GR 907303) will push you up onto the peat of the moor. Due east will take you up onto the ridge and the track along the county boundary. The more adventurous will want to strike out for the highest point, Hoof Stones Height (479m, 1,574 ft), on a bearing of about 155°. This is a steady plod through eroding peat haggs with only grouse and curlew for company. Unless it is very clear the compass is a necessity. The top is marked by a trig pillar; just north is a very obvious old boundary stone. The map marks others but few are now easily found.

From Hoof Stones Height follow the boundary ridge northwards through, at best, damp peat (sadly eroded in many places by motorbikes) and admire the views in both directions. After the long ridge of Black Hameldon you will drop more steeply to a low col with Cant Clough Reservoir to the left and Gorple Upper Reservoir to the right and then climb briefly to the shelter of the Hare Stones. Not a hare but a cock wheatear drew my attention to the massive cut millstone lying on their western side.

There is now a quite gentle climb up to the track below the Gorple Stones; unfortunately, though the moor here is clearly generally drier than on Black Hameldon, one of the wettest patches on the route lurks for the unwary. At the

Calderdale Countryside Service sign (which marks the boundary and warns that Gorple Gate is a bridleway only) you will probably not resist the short scramble up amongst the Gorple Stones themselves.

Return to the track and walk west for 2.5 km (1.6 miles), savouring the view as you do so. A memorial seat eases the weary as Hurstwood Reservoir comes in view down Smallshaw Clough. Some more old workings are obviously used by bikers here and it is presumably from this point that some of them get on to the moor.

Just beyond the gate, at the top of the brow alongside the first green intake off the moor, is a path to the left. Take this and drop to skirt along the upper edge of a pine plantation. Descend past the dam and enter the hamlet of Hurstwood. Alternative parking is available here at a NWW picnic site with toilets.

At the bottom corner of the picnic site use the gate to enter the Rock Water Valley. Shortly, find the footbridge at the start of the hazel and alder wood and cross and climb the bank to a track. Turn left, walk through the farm of Crow Holes and climb slowly to Middle Pasture. The view east over the moor is now uncluttered by power lines. Keep to the track and drop left to a bridge in Sheddon Clough. Turn right before it and right again up the bank at the marker post. Go through the wall and follow it along what is marked on the map as Sheddon Plantation, though it appears to be almost entirely rhododendron! At an up-and-over stile make for the marker post on the brow and then half left to drop to the surfaced path which leads you back shortly to the car park.

Historical Notes

Hurstwood: The hamlet is of fine stone buildings, the small church recently renovated. Hurstwood Hall (or Townley House), dated 1579, and Spenser House (where Edmund

Spenser, author of 'The Faerie Queene', is thought to have lived for two years) are especially fine.

Sheddon Clough: The strange, contorted appearance of the workings here has an eeriness about it even on a bright and sunny day. This battered landscape was created by hushing for limestone blocks buried in the boulder clay and sands deposited after the last Ice Age. The limestone was used for making mortar and to improve the grazing on the moorland edge. Hushing was a method of extracting minerals and ores from near surface exposures by damming up water and releasing it suddenly, so washing away the lighter material and leaving the rest behind. Traces of the dams and channels can still be seen. Working took place between 1600 and 1800 and ended after the canal reached Burnley and it became possible to transport limestone from elsewhere more easily. The limestone was burnt on site in simple kilns, one of which has been reconstructed. A guide book to the site is available from local Information Centres.

Gorple Gate: A very obvious and well made trackway, this was one of the many packhorse routes which crossed the moors when trade depended on what a pony could carry on his back over ground too difficult for wheels. The earliest dateable ones go back to pre-Conquest days though some may have been old even then. Many still retain a laid causeway of stone flags — though not this stretch of Gorple Gate. A Trust exists to help preserve them: South Pennine Pack Horse Trails, The Barn, Mankinholes, Todmorden OL14 6HR. Tel 0706-815598.

Rossendale Moors

Introduction: My boyhood, in the Manchester conurbation, was spent in comparative ignorance of that great half circle of hills which lie north and east. The level of air pollution meant I could hardly ever see them, and quite literally, soured appreciation when I was taken there. They stand out today, wide to the sun in (relatively) clean air. The area of moorland lying to the west of the Bury/Burnley road is usually now referred to as the West Pennine Moors. East of the road it is called, rather illogically, the South Pennines, and Rossendale makes up the south-western corner. This walk begins in Rawtenstall, before striking up to join the Rossendale Way. This area is a treasurehouse of our industrial past, particularly of quarrying, and the route leads past fascinating remnants of old workings, as well as giving excellent views over the Rossendale Valley. The walk also visits the best example in Lancashire of an 18th century loomshop, where handloom weavers worked and lived before the advent of the factory system.

Distance: The whole round is 15.6 km (9.7 miles) and can readily be extended into a longer day if wished. Maps — OS Landranger 103 & 109, OS Pathfinder 690 & 701.

Refreshments: Cafes, restaurants and pubs are avilable in Rawtenstall and The Buck at Cowpe is on the route.

How to get there: I suggest starting at the car park across from the Tourist Information Centre in Rawtenstall which is free.

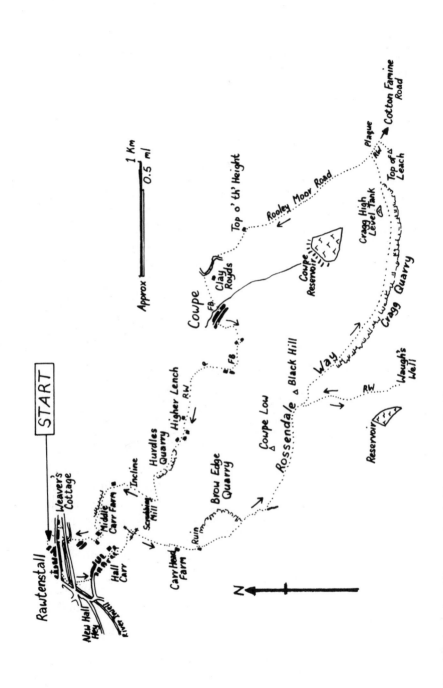

It gives the chance to use public transport if you want, and also allows you to stock up on refreshments and background should you wish (GR 814227).

The Walk: Take Bacup Road west past the bus station to the Methodist church. Turn left along the Limy Water and cross Bocholt Way into the ASDA car park; at the rear is a path up the bank onto Hall Carr Road. At the top of the estate bear right at Hall Carr Farm and through a small wood. Go immediately left on the far side and up the fence line to a gate on the track and turn right to a stile (GR 815220). Contour south along a flagstone fence boundary. Cross the wall and continue past the top side of Carr Head farm to join the track. Bear left at the bend and go left of the ruined house and barns and left up the track below the spoil of Brow Edge Quarry. At the top of the quarry aim for a gate in the wall and join the Rossendale Way. Pass through the first gate and go left of the wall before the second to cross onto the old tramway track. Take the yellow arrowed path left to follow round the south side of Cowpe Low. Right, across the valley, is a view of Holcombe Tower and ahead is Black Hill, stripped of vegetation and soil by motorcycle scrambling.

Stay with the tramway to the bottom of Black Hill (GR 857203), deviate right along the wall and contour 15 minutes to reach Waugh's Well. The view ahead is of Whittle Pike and far to the west you should be able to make out Darwen Tower. Return to the bottom of Black Hill and climb right. At the top of the hill the Rossendale Valley is spread out below with Bacup at the eastern end, and Pendle Hill bulks over the Forest of Rossendale to the north.

The Rossendale Way follows obvious tracks through the spoil of Cragg Quarry, with Cowpe Reservoir below to the left, and forks right at the far end above the water of Cragg High Level Tank. Aim for the stone gate posts at the junction of tramways and turn right to the plaque which commemorates the opening of the Rossendale Way on 28th April 1985. A permitted path behind takes you to the Top of Leach, a trig point, and an indicator stone erected by Jonathan Barcroft, of Horncliffe Quarries, in 1974. On a really clear day the Peak District is visible 20 miles to the south, and Ingleborough 35 miles north. If you have the time, it is worth an extra diversion to walk on for a while towards the county boundary over the 'Cotton Famine Road' laid as setts in the 1860s. Return to the plaque.

Turn north-west now and drop steadily down Rooley Moor Road. The whole length of Cragg Quarry now becomes visible to the left. Go through the moor gate and as far as the masts on the right. Turn left on the path in the field on the left of the buildings of Top o' th' Height farm. Follow the surfaced Water Works access road to a right-angled bend and take the gate on the left. Descend straight down a very wet and muddy path to cross the stream and emerge almost opposite The Buck in Cowpe. As you go you will pass Clay Royds farm to the left, where clay for the reservoirs was dug in the early 1900s, and Tenterheads Cottages to the right, where cloth was once left to bleach in the sun. Pass The Buck, go left in 20m and climb the track to houses to join a maze of paths along the valley side.

Go between the houses and right behind them to a water trough. Pick up an old paved path bearing left across the field to a bridge and kissing gate. Bear up left to another kissing gate and pass in front of the garages to join a built-up grassed track. At the sycamore tree, contour left round the hill on an ill-defined path to meet a very clear path coming up from Waterfoot down to your right; the Rossendale Way again. Keep to the clear path along an old wall line and contour over stiles to go above a rebuilt house. Walk straight through to the track up to Higher Lench and follow this up through the buildings to an old, flagged track through Hurdles Quarry.

At the fingerpost turn right onto the site of the former scrubbing mill.

Descend the bank steeply using the dismantled incline. Turn left at the second wall (GR 820221) and go left of the refurbished house to the end of the garden fence. Contour left now under the telephone lines to a stile by an ash tree on top of a small cliff. Follow the top of the cliff and drop down to a stile and an unmade lane, turn left and go round Middle Carr farm. Drop right downslope to the first building on the left and turn right on the track as far as the garages. Take the path between the top house and the last garage and drop down through a woodland nature reserve to emerge on Bocholt Way, at the bottom of Fallbarn Road beside an Irwell Way sign. Cross the river and road and walk through Tomlinson's car park to the Civic Trust office in the Weavers Cottage at Fallbarn Fold. Turn left to walk 100m beside the cricket ground back to the start.

Historical Notes

Countryside Centre: The Groundwork Trust operates a Countryside Centre at New Hall Hey just along to the right beyond ASDA. In the centre of the site is the distinctive Italianate chimney of Hardman Mill. There are exhibitions, events, refreshments, trails etc here. Tel 0706-211421. The East Lancashire Railway operates from Bury to Rawtenstall beside the Countryside Centre at weekends; Tel 061-764-7790.

Quarrying: The whole Rossendale area is a treasurehouse of the industrial past. A whole range of industries have come and gone here — wool, cotton, felt, footwear, coal, bricks, fireclay, lead — and some still remain, together with modern additions. The booklet 'The Changing Faces of Rossendale; Production Lines' contains an industrial trail around Cowpe, through which the route passes, which picks up many examples. More than any other industry, however, this route links together the remains of quarrying.

The moorlands are developed on rocks of the millstone grit series of carboniferous age, some 320 million years old. The coarsest material lies at the top, and occurs only at the top of the highest of the quarries which this route does not visit. The best of the rock, with fine, even grain size and very tough is found amongst the Haslingden Flags in quarries like Brow Edge, Cragg and Hurdles. These produced especially good paving, or flag, stones. Other quarries specialised in setts, kerbs and window sills, and there were a multitude of other less specialised products — roof stones, gateposts, wall stone, hearthstones and so on. Examples of part finished products can be found scattered around Cragg Quarry and a wander round any of the older parts of the built-up areas in Rossendale will reveal the inventive uses to which stone was put. Today, only a little working goes on, and this for broken rock for hardcore, aggregate etc.

Many stretches of the route still show the parallel grooved long blocks of stone used for the bed of tramways which transported the stone from the quarries. At the incline (GR 820221) wagons were hauled up and lowered to the main line by cable. On the more level ground a small steam engine hauled them, 20 at a time, on a three ft gauge track. Not only was the stone itself hauled but, of course, there was a need to remove overburden and waste too. The remains at the head of the incline are of the Scrubbing Mill where stone was cut and polished.

Waugh's Well: Built in 1866 as a memorial to the dialect writer and poet Edwin Waugh (1817–90). He often stayed at the nearby Foe Edge farm, now in ruins (GR 828197). Two other memorials have since been added — one to Ward Ogden, the other to Harry Craven.

Weavers' Cottages: On route at GR 815227 is the best example in Lancashire of an 18th century loomshop, which provided space for handloom weavers on the well-lit upper floor and formerly had living accommodation behind. It represents a stage between cottage industry and the factory system. It now serves as a base for the Rawtenstall Civic Society. Opening times are Saturday and Sunday, 2.00–5.00pm.

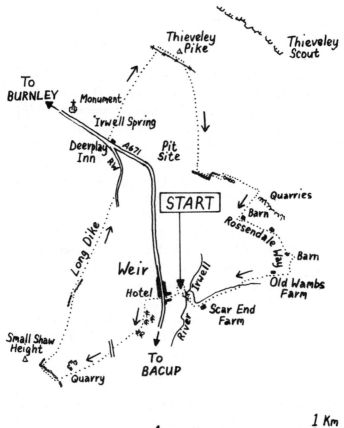

The Upper Irwell Valley

Introduction: Throughout most of its length the river Irwell is condemned to an urban setting but the valley above Bacup gives some impression of what Rossendale must have been like in the past. The very head of the valley, at Thieveley Pike, is as wild a spot as you could wish and yet within touching distance of habitation. Even in the late 20th century, driving rain or thick mist on this small moor can be dangerous and a compass is essential in such weather. The walk concentrates on getting a view of the valley from all angles and looking out from its western and northern boundaries.

Distance: A half day round of just over 8 km (5 miles) with a stiffish climb up the valley side and at least one section of hard going over purple moor-grass. Maps — OS Landranger 103, OS Pathfinder 690.

Refreshments: There are two pubs on the route; one in Weir, the Weir Hotel, and the other just below Thieveley Pike, The Deerplay. Additional refreshment is available in Bacup, including some fine fish and chips.

How to get there: Use the A671 from Burnley or Bacup to Weir and turn down Weir Street towards the river and a small parking area for the Irwell Valley Way (GR 872252).

The Walk: Walk back up to the main road and cross to the left of the Weir Hotel on a track as far as the first gate. Take the path left along the top of a field and above a new plantation, and go diagonally right to the top of a group of sycamore trees. Continue the line up by a fence and wall to exit onto a narrow lane. Cross this, continue the same line across a gully and bear right up the field to a stile by a small quarry. Turn right on the far side of the next wall to reach the trig point on Small Shaw Height. Cross back over the wall and follow the left-hand boundary roughly north-north-east to meet a track at GR 862251. Continue ahead to follow the Long Dike with the wall first on your left and then the right. Shortly after going below the power line, exit onto Bacup Old Road and follow this down to The Deerplay using a short section of the Rossendale Way in the process.

Just left of the pub a sign points up the moor. Use the path directly ahead, leaving the Irwell Spring to your left, to the crest of the grass moor. Bear right and reach the trig point on top of Thieveley Pike. Due north you look down over the scar of Thieveley Scout and to Holme Chapel down in the bottom of Cliviger; here were lead mines in the 17th century. Just beyond the trig point take the stile to the right and, ignoring the obvious path half left, bear off at 175° to cross the tussocks of moor grass to drop to a stile over a fence and wall. Go down the middle of the field to the bottom wall and turn left along the nearside to a stile in the corner and climb the field to a white gate. Go through, continue on the line of the wall to a good, new, arrowed stile on the right and drop down by the side of quarries to a track by a barn.

Turn left and follow the track past a house at the bottom of the quarries to a gateway just past a barn on the right. Leave the Rossendale Way by bearing right on the track and. walk down through the yard in front of the house of Old Wambs Farm and under the power lines again. Where the track bears right go ahead and pass an old dam on your left. Use the path on the left or keep on the track to the right of the clough to a kissing gate below Scar End farm. Turn right on the Irwell Valley Way and drop to cross the infant river and return to the start.

Historical Notes

Coal Mining: Before the railway came to Rossendale the population was dependent upon fuel obtained locally. At first this was wood and peat but from about 300 years ago coal was increasingly used. To begin with coal was won by simple bell pits dug into seams close to the surface, perhaps just serving individual farms or hamlets. Later the mines served the steam boilers of the mills and there was sufficient demand in the 19th century for new pits to be sunk. As the route circuits from Deerplay round over Thieveley Pike the old Deerplay Pit site is obvious in the dip below and the sad remains of an access road, with lamp standards still in place, can be seen below the pub: it closed in 1968. One small mine continues to operate, down in the valley to the left as you walk along the Long Dike, at Grime Bridge above Water.

War memorial: North-west of the Deerplay Inn (GR 862267) is a cross surmounting a large built-up plinth, all in some very non-local granite, and which is visible from a wide area around. It is a memorial to the men of Weir and Facit who died in the First World War and reads 'Lest we Forget'. When I last visited it was falling apart.

Cliviger gorge: On the way to or from this walk it is worth a diversion by car to drive the A646 Burnley–Todmorden road. The valley in the region of Holme Chapel and below the cliffs of Thieveley Scout is impressive but such stream as it has is clearly not big enough to have created such scenery. Standing atop Thieveley Pike looking down makes this even more apparent. The explanation is that the valley was formed towards the end of the Ice Age when it became the escape route for a much larger flow of water otherwise trapped by remnants of melting glacier ice — a classic example of a glacial meltwater channel.

Forest of Rossendale: Even today the map of the area north of the Rossendale Valley bodly bears the words 'Forest of Rossendale'. Originally the forest was the largest part of the Forest of Blackburnshire which also included Pendle, Trawden and Little Bowland. It ran from Accrington and Blackburn in the north to the river Irwell in the south, and from Hoddlesdon by Darwen in the west to the Irwell valley above Bacup in the east. Initially it was a genuine forest, that is to say an area in which the Royal laws of the forest applied — not necessarily an area wholly covered in trees. The writ of forest law ended in the early 16th century.

Within a medieval forest the king kept to himself all rights in respect of the 'vert' (the trees and associated items) and the 'venison' (the beasts of the forest), and punishment for infringement of the law could be harsh indeed. Today, such absolutism on the part of the monarch seems strange and I wonder whether much of the antagonism to landowners who are restrictive of public access does not derive from our legally forested past. Forests, however, were not entirely a dog-in-a-manger arrangement on the part of medieval kings. They did serve sensible purposes too. Kings did, after all, have to carry out a whole range of building works and needed timber for that purpose. They were also often on the move with no real fixed abode, and they and their followers had to be fed; and was the relaxation of the hunt really so much different in its effect from many modern recreations?